Innovation in Architecture

Innovation in Architecture

Edited by Alan J. Brookes and Dominique Poole

Spon Press
Taylor & Francis Group

LONDON AND NEW YORK

First published 2004 by Spon Press
11 New Fetter Lane, London EC4P 4EE

Simultaneously published in the USA and Canada
by Spon Press
29 West 35th Street, New York, NY 10001

Spon Press is an imprint of the Taylor and Francis Group

Typeset in Univers by Ninety Seven Plus
Printed and bound in Spain by Grafos

British Library Cataloguing in Publication Data
A catalogue record for this book is available from the British Library

Library of Congress Cataloging in Publication Data
Innovation in architecture / edited by Alan J. Brookes and Dominique
Poole.
     p. cm.
ISBN 0-415-24133-2 (softcover : alk. paper)
1. Architecture and technology. 2. Architecture--Technological
innovations. 3. Building materials. I. Brookes, Alan J. II. Poole,
Dominique.
NA2543.T43I56 2003
721'.09'04--dc21
                         2002154951

ISBN 0-415-24133-2

Contents

List of Contributors

Professor Alan J. Brookes has an international reputation as an architect and technology consultant over the last 23 years since his involvement with Heathrow Terminal 4. Unusually he has combined practice with a continual educational role over the same period. Previously a partner in Brookes Stacey Randall he has worked with Atelier One on the Singapore Arts Centre and Melbourne Federation Square.

More recently he acted as expert witness on the glazing at Waterloo International Station and as consultant to Manchester Airport Interchange. His educational responsibilities include Visiting Professor at Oxford Brookes and Singapore Universities. He was guest Professor of Wohnbau at Aachen University 1999 to 2001 and is now Professor of Architecture and Building Technology at Delft TU. His books include Concepts of Cladding, Cladding of Buildings, Building Envelope and Connections.

Dr Dominique Poole studied Architecture at Oxford Brookes University and received a PhD for her thesis on technical innovation from the clients' perspective in 2002. Her research, carried out with Buro Happold, provides an understanding of issues that influence client decisions regarding innovative practices and solutions and the implications of these for those involved in the construction process.

She has experience of project based learning within the construction industry and has analysed the effectiveness of communities of practice. She has particular expertise in the fields of technical innovation and knowledge management, which is currently being applied at Arup Research and Development.

Julia Barfield MBE RIBA studied at the Architectural Association. She co-founded MarksBarfield Architects in 1989. The practice has received over twenty-five awards for excellence including the Architectural Practice of the Year Award in 2001. In 2000 she was made an MBE in the Queen's New Year's Honours List and was awarded the Prince Philip Special Commendation for Outstanding Achievement in Design for Business and Society. She lectures widely at universities, schools, educational conferences and institutions such as the RIBA, Royal Academy of Arts, and Royal Institution in London, and for the British Council overseas. She has been a judge for both the RIBA and Civic Trust and is a Council Member of the Architectural Association.

Chris Clarke was born in Sheffield in 1948. He emigrated to Australia and then returned to London to complete his architectural studies at the Polytechnic of Central London in 1969. He worked as an associate with John Winter and Associates (1974–82) then with Norman Foster (1982–3) on the Hongkong Shanghai Bank and Stansted Airport. He returned to Brisbane in 1984 and became master architect for Expo '88. Since becoming a principal of Bligh Voller Nield in 1993 he has been responsible for the design of the new Brisbane International Airport Terminal (1995); the Ansett Terminal, Sydney (2000); Stadium Australia, Sydney (1999) and various other projects.

Alan J. Brookes
Dominique Poole
Julia Barfield
Chris Clarke

Mike Cook studied Mechanical Sciences at Cambridge University followed by a PhD at Bath University. Mike joined Buro Happold in 1982, becoming a partner in 1994. He is a Chartered Engineer and Member of the Institution of Structural Engineers.

Mike Cook is a creative individual whose heart lies in the structural design of buildings. He is happiest developing an integrated picture of a building along with an architect. Projects in which he has played a principal role include: Natural History Museum, Kensington; Community College, Hackney; Canopies for Sainsbury, Canterbury; City Technical College, Bristol; Imagination Building, London. Worldwide: Music Pavilion, Baltimore, USA; CFAN Mobile Arena, Harare, Zimbabwe; Cultural Forum Baghdad, Iraq; Headquarters office tower for RWE, Essen, Germany. Mike was resident engineer for the cable net roof of the Tsim Sha Shui Cultural Centre, Hong Kong.

Mike Davies has worked with the Richard Rogers Partnership for over thirty years and has been involved with all projects carried out by the practice. He worked for six years in Paris on the Pompidou Centre and was Project Architect for the Institute for Research and Co-ordination in Acoustics and Music (IRCAM). On returning to the UK he worked on the Lloyd's of London project, on Inmos, the Government microprocessor industry flagship.

His particular roles within the partnership include responsibility for urban design, technology, scientific research and development. He was Project Director for the strategic masterplans of the Royal Docks in London and for masterplans of the City of Dunkirk, for Leamouth and the Greenwich Peninsula in London. He is the project Director for Terminal 5 at Heathrow Airport and Riverside Towers at Canary Wharf. He was awarded a CBE in 2000 for services to architecture.

Richard Horden worked with Foster Associates from 1975 – 1985. Just before the Hong Kong and Shanghai Bank was under construction he left to start his own practice in London, Richard Horden Associates in parallel with Horden Cherry Lee, and is now working as a Professor in Architecture and Product Design at T.U. Munich specialising in advanced lightweight architecture and space technology.

Mike Cook
Mike Davies
Richard Horden

Tony Hunt has wide experience in building structures of all types and in all materials, but his speciality is primarily in sophisticated steelwork, working closely with most of the leading architects in the UK and also in France. He is first and foremost a designer, believes in offering a structural philosophy parallel to architects and is actively involved in the design development of projects. He set up Anthony Hunt Associates in 1962.

Eva Jiricna is director of Eva Jiricna Architects (EJA), an architectural and design practice based in London with an international portfolio of residential, commercial and retail interiors, furniture, products and exhibitions, and private and public buildings. The practice is at the forefront of innovation in form and technology, with highly crafted and detailed designs employing classic materials – glass, steel and stone – in a thoroughly modern language. As a multi-disciplinary practice, EJA provides a comprehensive service including the design of new buildings and public spaces as well as detailed interiors, products and furniture.

David Kirkland studied architecture at the Royal College of Art, London and at the Illinois Institute of Technology in Chicago.

Presently David divides his time between contributing to the Grimshaw office where he is engaged in developing their sustainability agenda and establishing his own innovation-led design studio, David Kirkland + Associates where he is currently developing innovative design solutions for energy and resource efficient buildings and products. His designs include buildings, bridges, exhibitions, furniture and products.

David has taught architecture and has a deep interest in nature and its design process. He is currently working on a documentary programme aimed at communicating this to a wider audience.

Mark Lovell is a chartered engineer and is now principal of Mark Lovell Design Engineers (MLDE), a design engineering consultancy based in Wiltshire, UK. He has worked for high-profile consultancy practices and has engineered many award-winning landmark buildings and innovative structures. His projects range from huge mobile cranes to buildings and façade systems, many of which have been protected by patent. He intuitively promotes the integration of design and manufacture to create efficient solutions to client briefs. He has a keen interest in environmental and sustainable issues and in contributing to the ongoing development of strategic ideas and working methods.

Tony Hunt
Eva Jiricna
David Kirkland
Mark Lovell

Luke Lowings was born in Cambridge in 1961. After studying as an architect and working in London (for the Richard Rogers Partnership among others), he moved to New York in 1989 and for twelve years worked as a collaborator in the studio of sculptor James Carpenter, testing the relationship of light, structure and material in architecture. During that period he became a registered architect in the UK and New York State and taught at the University of Philadelphia, New Jersey Institute of Technology and Columbia University in New York. In 2001 he returned to Europe, setting up a partnership with Carpenter in London to continue their explorations.

Volkwin Marg Born in 1936 in Königsberg. Since 1965 freelance architect together with Meinhard von Gerkan. Fled to West-Berlin 1956. Architectural studies in Berlin and Brunswick in 1958. Many competition successes and large projects, lectures and manuscripts on architecture, urban planning and political culture. Fritz Schumacher Award 1996. Appointment to the Chair of Town Planning and Tradesmanship, RWTH Aachen 1997.

David Marks studied at the Architectural Association. In 1989 he co-founded MarksBarfield Architects with Julia Barfield. In 1994 they founded the London Eye Company and as managing director he raised all of the necessary finance for the development. The Millennium Wheel has become a new symbol for London and the most popular attraction in the UK. In 2000 he was made an MBE in the Queen's New Year's Honours List and was awarded the Prince Philip Special Commendation for Outstanding Achievement in Design for Business and Society. In 2001 he was awarded the Faculty of Building Trophy for outstanding work in the field of construction. The practice received the Architectural Practice of the Year Award in 2001.

Chris Wilkinson founded Wilkinson Eyre Architects in 1983 and has built it up to become one of the leading architectural practices in the country. He has directed a large number of the practice's key projects, including the Stirling Prize-winning Gateshead Millennium Bridge and Magna Project. He was awarded an OBE in 2003 for services to architecture.

Luke Lowings
Volkwin Marg
David Marks
Chris Wilkinson

Picture credits

Ludwig Abache 7.1, 7.2

Architeckten von Gerkan, Marg and Partner 12.1, 12.5, 12.6

Arup 7.6, 7.7, 10.6

Brecht-Einzig/Arcaid Architectural Photography Picture Library 2.8

Brookes Stacey Randall 1.3

Buro Happold 7.3, 7.8, 7.9, 7.10, 7.11

Carpenter/Lowings Architecture and Design 10.13, 10.14, 10.15

Peter Cook 4.8, 6.7

Mike Davies 1.4, 2.6, 2.7, 2.10

Ana-Maria D'Costa 7.4, 7.5

Peter Durant/arcblue.com 1.5

Richard Du Toit 4.4

Diana Edmunds 13.1, 13.15

K Frahm 12.7

Dennis Gilbert 8.10, 8.14, 8.15, 13.3, 13.4, 13.13, 13.14

Brian Gulick 10.1, 10.2, 10.3, 10.4, 10.5

Guy Hearn, photo used with kind permission from Gateshead Council 13.11

Andrew Holt 6.8, 6.9

Richard Horden 8.1, 8.2, 8.4, 8.5, 8.12, 8.16

Richard Horden/Mira Esposito 8.6

Institute for Lightweight Structures, University of Stuttgart 10.6

JCDA Inc. 10.7, 10.9, 10.10, 10.11, 10.12

Eva Jiricna 9.1, 9.2, 9.3, 9.4

Katsuhisa Kida 2.1, 2.2

David Kirkland 4.1, 4.3, 4.7, 4.16

Ken Kirkwood 2.9

Heiner Leiska 12.2, 12.3, 12.4

Mark Lovell 5.1, 5.2, 5.3, 5.4, 5.5, 5.6, 5.7, 5.8, 5.9, 5.10, 5.11, 5.12, 5.13, 5.14, 5.15, 5.16, 5.17

Dan MacCarrie/Melon Studios 13.10

MarksBarfield Architects 6.1, 6.3, 6.4, 6.5, 6.6

James Morris 13.5, 13.6, 13.7

Stephen Morris 5.0

NASA/Jim Moran 4.5

Nasa 4.6

Nicholas Grimshaw & Partners Ltd 4.9, 4.10, 4.11, 4.12, 4.13, 4.14, 4.15

Eamon O'Mahony 8.3, 8.8

Richard Rogers Partnership Library 2.5

Christian Richters 2.3

Albert Scharger 8.13

Jürgen Schmidt 12.1

Tim Soar 13.16

Harry Sowden, Arup 2.4

Morley von Sternberg (www.vonsternberg.com) 13.9

Dan Stevens 2.0

D'Arcy Thompson (*On Growth and Form*) 6.2

Wilkinson Eyre Architects 13.8, 13.12

Adam Wilson 13.2

Nick Wood 6.0

Chapter 1

Introduction

Alan J. Brookes and Dominique Poole

The doctor can bury his mistakes but an architect can only advise his clients to plant vines.

Frank Lloyd Wright,
New York Times Magazine, 4 October 1953

The dictionary definition of 'innovate' is to introduce new things or methods into established practice. Invention can be considered as the process of discovering or creating a novel idea, while innovation is the application or exploitation of an idea. Innovation also differs from invention in being achieved through a deliberate application of knowledge.

The issues relating to innovations in new materials and the technology utilized in their application are complex. Innovations in building materials are by no means a simple process. Marian Bowley describes a process consisting of three main stages.[1] Initially the new material is invented or introduced. This is followed by a period in which use becomes established, which may include changes to improve performance. Finally different varieties of the original material may be developed. This book mainly includes examples where architects and engineers have introduced innovation as part of their bespoke designs for a building project.

Jean Prouvé has discussed a deficiency of architectural inspiration in relation to the new materials that mechanization has put at our disposal. He suggests that this is partly due to a lack of courage, a quality fundamental to a change in attitudes towards innovation in design. He was not alone in this observation. More recently Peter Rice has written of courage as the missing ingredient in the process of design development:

> The courage you need is the courage to start. Once launched, then each step can be evolved naturally. Each step requires careful examination. The courage to start and an unshakeable belief in one's ability to solve the new problems which will arise in the development are essential.[2]

The various contributors to this book have shown in their own work their willingness to be involved in this innovative process and to face the risks involved.

The idea for the book stemmed from research into innovation at Oxford Brookes University leading to Dominique Poole's PhD thesis. Some of the contributors were present at a conference at the Illinois Institute of Technology in Chicago in 1999, organized by Professor Peter Land, at which delegates were invited to show their work in a critical way – exhibiting not just the end result but also the difficult process by which they achieved their aims –

and to compare new ways of dealing with materials and building techniques. The book has therefore concentrated on the exploration and development of the ideas driving architectural solutions rather than on an appraisal of the end results and it is assumed that the reader will already be familiar with most of the projects described by the various authors.

Perhaps we should first investigate why architects and engineers use materials in an innovative manner and produce innovative structural solutions. They may simply be responding to the opportunities offered by new materials and the more sophisticated means of prediction now available to them. Alternatively, it may be, as Martin Pawley argues, that architects have lost their ability to control traditional technology and that control can only be regained by recognizing and transferring advanced techniques from other industries to architecture.[3]

There may be additional sources for technological change. Nature has always had a profound influence on architecture in both aesthetic and functional terms. For centuries people have looked to nature for an understanding of process or indeed for inspiration. Peter Buchanan has written about the natural influence behind Renzo Piano's Menil Museum.

> For architecture or technology to emulate nature neither necessitates nor excludes using natural materials and vernacular, or biomorphic forms. But as science unravels nature's secrets, it is the leading edge of technology, which some may mistake for its most artificial and unnatural pole, that is most likely faithfully to appropriate nature, especially in artefacts expressly created for some high performance application. This artefact or component may have biomorphic form, not because it is styled that way, but because it happens to offer the economy, efficiency and exact fit for purpose found in organic creation.[4]

In learning from nature the ultimate goal is an architecture that responds to the environment. David Kirkland, Marks Barfield, Eva Jiricna and Volkwin Marg (Chapters 4, 6, 9 and 12) all refer to their interest in scientific discovery and the influence of forms in nature.

An idea often promoted within architecture is that of technology transfer, where a vast technology exists outside the construction industry and the architect acts as 'active forager', as bridgehead or a technology-transfer mechanism from these other sectors. This is not necessarily the case, however. Our belief is that technology actively exists within the present building industry. This resource is playing a more significant part in modern architecture as a result of a change in attitudes towards construction and its effect on design. This idea is reinforced by Professor Beukers of the Faculty of Aerospace Engineering at Delft University of Technology, who believes that the aerospace industry is relatively conservative compared to the British building industry and indeed looks to us for a sense of innovation.[5]

Many of this book's contributors admit to an early interest in the mechanisms of how things are put together. Volkwin Marg (Chapter 12) refers to his childhood in Danzig, where he had a keen interest in boats and the natural materials used in their construction. Tony Hunt (Chapter 3) describes how he was brought up on Meccano and became fascinated by powered model aircraft design while still at school. Mike Davies' amusing description (Chapter 2) of his time at the Architectural Association, his interest in pneumatics and the influence of his tutor, Ron Herron (Archigram), shows his early interest in alternative technology.

Peter Rice, in his book, *An engineer imagines*, comments:

> Exploration and innovation are the keys. I have noticed over the years that the most effective use of materials is often achieved when they are being explored and used for the first time. The designer does not feel inhibited by precedent.

Modern building with innovative forms and use of materials offers this opportunity for exploration. Each building is in effect a prototype and the building industry demands its particular method of design, testing and sourcing of materials.

Extreme environments may also act as a catalyst for innovation. Much in the way of new technology and materials used in construction was originally developed within the aerospace industry or by NASA, who are skilled in experimentation within extreme environments. The United States proposal to build a space station in the 1980s led to a research programme in deployable structures funded by

1.1
Natural forms: the spider's web

1.2
Deployable systems may be developed through origami and mathematics

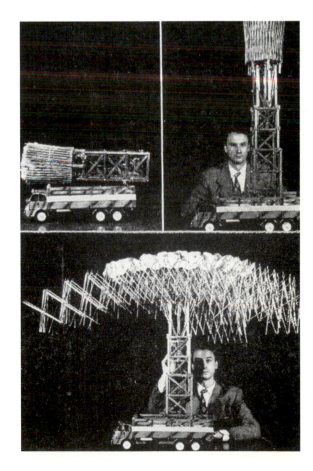

NASA.[6] Richard Horden (Chapter 8) is clearly influenced by his knowledge of alternative technologies and by his work as Professor of Architecture in Munich on crew habitation units for NASA.

The introduction of these unfamiliar technologies raises the issue of risk and the consequential professional indemnity requirements. Architects generally accept a responsibility to their client and may be reluctant to utilize a new technique until evidence exists to support its success. Thus a critical consideration behind the ability to innovate is the available capacity to design, prototype and test. Only through these means is confidence in a new product or method of construction established. Architects keen to explore frontiers of design and innovation are forced to carry out experimental models, often at their own expense, to prove their ideas will work in practice.

Generally, in any other manufacturing industry, the first project utilizing a new method of construction or application of a new material would be seen as a prototype. However, buildings by their nature are often intended for longevity of use so defects and long-term durability are determined only after significant time has passed. British standards and codes can be used as a datum point for established materials, but such guides are unlikely to be available for new methods, furthering the level of risk involved. Additionally, architects are often required to work to tight schedules and these may simply not allow for an exploration of an innovative method, forcing them to make do with an established material or method of construction. Quantity surveyors' costing methods are also based on tried and tested solutions, where general judgements are based on past experience and knowledge.

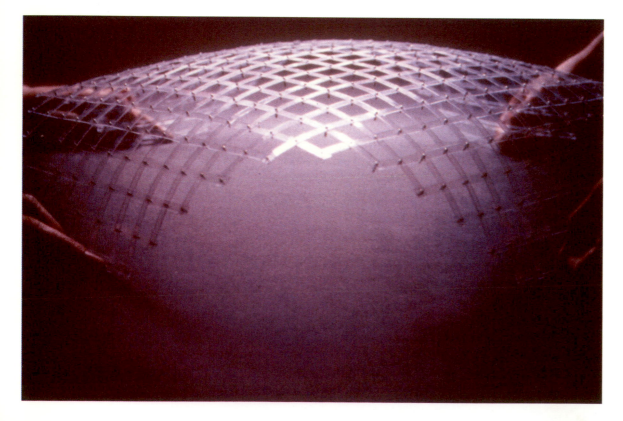

1.3
Computers and models extensively simulate practical circumstances: experimental model of an aluminium grid shell (architect: Brookes Stacey Randall, 1993)

1.4
The Pompidou 'gerberettes' being hoisted into position (architect: Richard Rogers and Renzo Piano)

In order to design within a new process it is important for the architect or engineer to know the limitations of that process. In the development of the Pompidou *gerberettes* the design team made visits to foundries to gain a better insight into the limitations of cast steel. As Peter Rice explains,

> When innovating, which using cast steel in this way was, it is essential to have detailed and thorough analysis facilities available from highly skilled people with no emotional commitment to making the solution work, just a clear, logical and objective insistence that the structure and its materials satisfy all the laws and requirements they should.

Cast steel was a poorly understood material, having a craft-based background dating from the nineteenth century that had failed to evolve. This prompted a new technology to be introduced in order to test the pieces successfully. At the time, fracture mechanics was emerging in other industries, prompted by the need for reliable steel jackets for nuclear reactors and by the complexity of constructing oil platforms for the North Sea. Fracture mechanics is the science of predicting the behaviour of metals under strain and how they would react if small flaws and cracks existed within them. The Pompidou team were able to benefit from this knowledge to cast the

gerberettes – an example of technology transfer, where an existing technology from one industry is utilized within another. Although this was the process through which the *gerberettes* were finally produced, the marriage of a traditional craft process and the innovative method of fracture mechanics did not initially prove successful because of a failure in communication.

In a similar way Eva Jiricna (Chapter 9) describes how the slight difference in size between Czech and British metric screws nearly caused a failure in the construction of her Orangery in Prague. Eva is renowned for her ability to utilize glass as a construction material but remains pessimistic about the prospects for advanced technology, as the cost of tooling up new components can never be covered by the return on any single project. On the subject of the glass staircase for her client Joseph Ettedgui she says. 'We use it as a structural material; not placed on top of something as a surface but as a replacement for metal or wood. It is only possible because there are no faults in glass: it's very homogenous.' Interestingly, the first edition of *New ways of building* by Eric de Maré contains an illustration of glass stairs dating from 1937. They form the entrance of the St Gobain Glass Pavilion of the Paris Exhibition.[7]

The projects reviewed in this book show there has been a considerable increase in the use of new materials and processes in the building industry. It is becoming more common for designers to be expected to extend their creativity into areas of which they may have imperfect understanding. Consequently the builder is expected to implement novel concepts while possessing equally limited knowledge and experience. In this circumstance there is always a danger that these unfamiliar techniques could lead to failure and there is an increasing demand for the architect to be diligent in this respect. The contributors to this book are fully aware of this responsibility.

In traditional construction, designer and contractor have access to a long-established body of knowledge of familiar building techniques and their limitations. An understanding of these processes can exist between the two parties and consequently the designer can confidently rely on the contractor to carry out minor on-site adjustments by cutting and fitting to 'make good'. Standard details are familiar to those involved in the trade and are relied upon as tried and tested methods. For example, a bricklayer instructed to build a wall of standard brick and blockwork construction with no specific request for wall ties would automatically know to include them in the appropriate places. As Mike Cooley points out: 'The craftsman's common sense is a vital form of knowledge which is acquired in that complex "learning by doing situation".'[8] The sequence of erection is understood and ideally each tradesman would work to a standard suitable to enable those following to carry out their task without having to correct the deficiencies of those previous. Therefore there exists a degree of autonomy in the construction process on which the designer tends to rely when designing the building details.

When new materials and methods of construction are introduced the dialogue between design and production may break down, as there is no existing common knowledge of the construction method. These new techniques imply an unfamiliar sequence of assembly or method of construction that may lead to a difficulty in recognizing problems inherent in the design. The introduction of factory-made prefabricated components does not normally allow site cutting or adjustments on site. The transition from craft-based to mechanized industry has led to the diminished role of the individual craftsman. Consequently craftsmen skilled in the traditional trades are becoming scarce. Craft has been transferred from the site to the manufacturing process.

For example, in the design of the glazing at the Lloyd's headquarters, Richard Rogers Partnership required treatment of the glass surface for environmental control. In conjunction with the curtain-wall suppliers, Josef Gartner, the practice developed the use of glass drops during the manufacturing process. Occasionally it may even be necessary for architects to interfere directly with the process of construction. At the Thames Water Tower, London, the architects, Brookes Stacey Randall, assisted with the sourcing of the suspended glass fittings and the bracketry because these were not available from conventional sources.

The relationship between design and production is different in the building industry to other industries. According to Pawley:

> The reason you get better products out of the car industry, aerospace and racing yacht design is because they are all businesses that depend on performance to succeed. In architecture success doesn't depend on performance but on value. To get better performance you need a lot of research and development – to get value you need only scarcity.[9]

Within the motor sport industry the relationship between the structural designer and the manufacturer is one that is well established and crucial to the implementation of the cutting-edge technology required to achieve high performance. Take, for example, the chassis of a Formula One car, which will be constantly redesigned and refined to perfect the ultimate lightweight component to provide the critical advantage in a race; in the building industry there is little opportunity for constant redesign and prototyping.

As Peter Rice understood through experience: 'Communication is the key to progress'. The communication of a design and its specification can become misunderstood when translated from one country to another. The manufacture of the *gerberettes* for the Pompidou illustrates this point particularly well. Following casting, the first steel

1.5
An innovative means of changing appearance, adapting existing technology: Thames Water Tower, London (architect: Brookes Stacey Randall, 1994)

gerberette underwent testing and failed at half the design load, as did the second one. The design team visited the German manufacturers, Krupps, to try to ascertain the reason for the failures. The explanation was a classic case of international misunderstanding. The tender had been written in French using French national standards as was required, except for one British standard that specified the material quality for the castings. Rice explains;

> It was a British standard because most of the work on this new approach in fracture mechanics had been simulated by the problems of making the North Sea oil platforms, and the British Standards Institute had perforce to define a way of measuring steel quality in these conditions.

The British standard was cross-referenced to a French standard in the early stages for the purpose of tender and consequently the German contractors substituted an equivalent German standard, assured that the German standards were more rigorous than the equivalent French. One may assume that once the problem had been identified it would be fairly easy to rectify but this was not the case. The Germans had faith in their own DIN standards, said to be the most rigorous and stringent, but little faith in the British standards. The problem was resolved only after the design team met with a respected German professor at Stuttgart University, Professor Kussmaul, who was familiar with fracture mechanics. After he explained that the British method was correct and a colleague of his discovered a method for reheating the pieces already made, the manufacturing process continued with success.

The practice of utilizing new materials today is far removed from traditional methods of experimentation. According to Rice:

> In the mid-nineteenth century materials were explored by building and waiting. Some of the structures built in this way would be difficult

to justify today with all our modern analysis techniques and our need to satisfy modern rules and norms on safety and soundness.

The risks are perhaps much greater and more forbidding today, and few are prepared to take them. Calculations can determine the required size and property needs of structure, while public safety is regarded high on the agenda of consideration for any structure.

Material developments in the twentieth century

As early as 1983 Jan Kaplicky and David Nixon of Future Systems were already speculating on the future of advanced composites:

> We will certainly be able to use them in the building industry for all sorts of advanced structural designs, but even now it would be possible to use them selectively. By combining carbon fibre with glass fibre in a structural I-beam profile, for example, we could carefully position the carbon fibres on the section extremities where they would do the most work.[10]

This ability to combine fibres and to predict, using computer technology, where they will be put to the best use within the structure creates unique opportunities for advanced composite construction. This prediction technique will enable structures to be produced more economically, applying more expensive fibres such as carbon only where they are required.

Chris McCarthy of Battle McCarthy suggests that architects could apply composites in prefabricated construction, where weight is critical in relation to transport costs.[11] He also believes the future of composite materials could exploit technology transfer from genetic engineering to form self-maintaining skins drawn from the precedent of the sea slug. It is certain that a greater scientific understanding of materials can only help inform their development:

1.6
Singapore Arts Centre, 1997: the complex roof form (architect: D.P. Architects)

'At present, the possibilities of detailing in composites have been unexplored, with the result that the structural form of composite construction is often bland and fails to express the qualities of the material or the technical achievement.'

Like the cast-iron bridge at Coalbrookdale, with its detailing that appeared as though it had been constructed from timber with dovetail joints, the early composite bridges that used pultruded sections were mechanically bolted together. It would have shown more integrity to exploit the seamless quality of the material. This problem of detailing is relevant to all new materials, many of which are applied in ways that reflect traditional methods of construction. The construction process inevitably undergoes a process of evolution until the new material is able to exhibit its unique sense of identity.

The role of the computer

Projects such as the façade for the Melbourne Federation Square Arts Centre and the Singapore Arts Centre would have been impossible to design without computers to handle the complicated geometry.[12]

The form of the concert hall and Lyric Theatre at the Singapore Arts Centre was ideally suited to computer-aided development, having a sculpted, non-linear surface.[13] A space-frame grid supports a glazed infill and aluminium shading devices and forms the complex surface form. The engineers responsible for the façade, Atelier One, in conjunction with DPA architects in Singapore, developed the concept using Microstation software to model the surface face geometry, creating a series of dimensionally equal elements to enable a more efficient and economical manufacture process.

The concept of computer-aided design was first introduced in the USA.[14] Britain began experimenting with interactive graphics in the 1960s using mainframe computers, but since the introduction of micro-computers in the early 1970s these techniques have advanced at a tremendous rate. Computer-aided manufacture works on the basis of CAD-produced tapes that numerically control machine tools by drawing cutting paths around a two-dimensional drawing. With the technology of computer-operated component machining and the development of mechanical handling and inspection machinery controlled by the same numerical method, the process of fully automatic manufacture is achievable. Despite the rate of technological advance, it is important to remember that the scale of growth is initially limited by the desire and capacity of people in the industry to adapt, and social factors are as important as the adoption of computing in the building industry.

Computer technology has perhaps played its most significant role in the design of complicated structures. Many complex forms formerly precluded by an inability to reproduce accurate models can now be modelled with ease and their structures may undergo rigorous testing before they become a reality. For example, the computer is now a critical tool in the design of tensile architecture. Martin Rowell explains:

> Tensile architecture is very much bounded
> by physics, and we have to be able to assure

the client it's going to work. With fabric shaping it's not always humanly possible to decide what will work and you have to go into computer analysis at an early stage.[15]

Prior to the availability of the appropriate software technology Frei Otto and Antonio Gaudí used hanging chain models to define forms of minimal energy. These are pure tension structures and the form can be inverted to form an optimal compression structure under uniform loads. The form of the timber lattice structure for the Mannheim Garden Festival was designed using these modelling techniques. When inverted this form generates a 'catenery' structure of pure compression under self-weight.

Computer models have three unique advantages over other forms of three-dimensional representation: first, they generate the shape of the structure; this in turn allows analysis of its behaviour under changing load conditions; and, finally, the exact detailed geometry of each component can be determined, enabling each part to be manufactured correctly first time and assembled with the other components to create the product.

A major application of computer technology is in the field of structural analysis. Engineers and architects can model in real terms some of the junctions and critical detail of their designs so that the physical reality of these designs can be observed (see 1.7). Equations required for analysis of the structure are put into the system and solved automatically upon request of the analytical output. Displacement, loads, shear and moments are all factors that can be predicted. Changes of input are easily facilitated and the corresponding result can be shown on request. This technological advance has proved to be indispensable in the design of complex forms and tensile architecture, allowing many complicated structures to become a reality and simultaneously reducing the factor of risk.

The computer software used in the form finding of tensile structures was originally developed in the

1.7
Singapore Arts Centre, 1997: a computer-generated image of the effect of wind loading

late 1960s and early 1970s. In conventional structures, the engineer's aim is to determine stresses through the testing of a trial form under a variety of loading conditions. This process is reversed in the shape determination of a tensile structure, as the stresses or prestresses are specified prior, and the designer can manipulate the computer model until the desired shape is formed. In addition, a coloured output on the computer screen indicates the degree to which all parts are stressed and if any areas are not under tension at all. These techniques enable a variety of alternative solutions to be investigated, such as different types of fabric, different numbers and positions of supports, and alternative shapes of boundaries to the membrane.

The latest computer-modelling methods are based on finite element analysis. Previously, innovative designs were constrained by the limitations of the analysis method. In contrast the only limitations now are those inherent to the properties of the materials and the designer's imagination. One of the most versatile and widely used structural-analysis programmes is called NASTRAN, originally developed by NASA's Goddard Space Flight Centre to aid aerospace vehicle design. It analyses a structural design and predicts how it will perform under different conditions. To achieve this, the object is dissected into a series of independent structural elements. Each element is individually analysed for stress and deflection and then compared with the adjoining element until the whole structure has been analysed.

Technology is advancing at a rapid rate and it is evident that computers will continue to become commonplace even in the smallest of practices. Technology is continually in a process of evolution and there are still many improvements to be made both in terms of technical capabilities and social consequences. Cooley reports that there still exists a belief that CAD systems fail to exploit the full potential of interactive computing, especially because

of human ability. He quotes Howard Rosenbrock, who believes that the human mind and the computer have different but complementary abilities. Where the human mind excels in pattern recognition, the assessment of complex situations and the intuition to form new solutions, the computer excels in analysis and numerical computation.

Often innovation can be attributed to the knowledge and experience acquired through a series of projects. Certain aspects of the design and construction of one project may inform the development of further projects. This point can be illustrated with examples of Michael Hopkins' built projects. The 'Patera' system, a prefabricated building system, can be seen to have influenced the essential plan of the factory for Schlumberger. In turn the Schlumberger project informed the design of the tensile roof structure at Lord's Cricket Ground. Experience of load-bearing brickwork at Lord's was then applied to the masonry construction at Glyndebourne and subsequently at the Inland Revenue Building in Nottingham. Eva Jiricna says that only a single innovation should be introduced on any one project.

Transfer of information can also exist within the profession itself. The employment structure of the building industry is such that many people from different disciplines are able to exchange ideas and learning with one another. It is not unusual for architects in practice to trade information with manufacturers who have specialist knowledge of their proposed method of assembly. Within practices there continues a trend for peer groups to share their specialist skills and exchange ideas and methods. This process is important as even established architects producing innovative designs return to the role of students learning from precedent. It is to be expected that when individual architects move from one practice to another they may take with them a certain design vocabulary and knowledge of the building process.

One of the disappointing factors of this information flow is that younger architects and engineers often fail to learn from the history of technology. In one of the studios at the School of Architecture at Delft University of Technology there is an original prototype piece from Jean Prouvé's medical facility in Rotterdam. Students of architecture and building technology pass it by hardly knowing of its significance in the development of formed metal composite cladding. Similarly, they would mostly have no knowledge of Konrad Wachsmann's seminal book *The turning point of*

building, structure and design, which shows the development of the component module and the amazing dynamic structure that could be achieved using the standardized form of a three-legged wishbone-like member.[16] However, there are still rare examples at the various schools of architecture of prototyping and testing of assemblies. At RWTH Aachen University, Jan Wurm and others continue to involve students in full-size testing of prototypes.

Strangely, the Building Industry seems slow to accept or develop new ideas. *New ways of building* by Eric de Maré (1948) referred to use of high-

1.8
Singapore Arts Centre, 1997: mock-up of sunshades (architect: DP Architects)

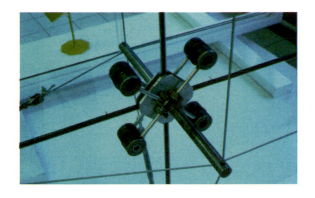

Experimental model for suspended glass panels by Professor Mick Eekhout, 1999

strength bond adhesives and lighter alloys that are hardly in use fifty years later. Despite the recently renewed interest in industrialized housing in the UK, those developing new systems may not be aware of the IBIS house and the pioneering work of the Consortia Building Programme so well described by Barry Russell in the book *Building systems, industrialization and architecture*.[17] The clever joint and panel system developed for the Patera system (see Tony Hunt chapter 3) remains largely ignored.

A vision of the future

However far modern science and technics have fallen short of their inherent possibilities they have taught mankind at least one lesson: nothing is impossible.

Technics and civilization
Mumford, Lewis (1963)
Harcourt Trade Publishers, New York

Primarily, architects have a responsibility to their clients and a tried and tested solution is often a better basis for those not prepared to take risks. Past unfavourable experience may cause individuals to be wary of a particular product or method of assembly. But it appears that much of the stigma associated with new methods could be dispelled if care was taken to gain familiarity with the manufacturing process and

understand the limitations of the material, enabling details to be designed with confidence. It is therefore important that professional bodies recognize the increased responsibility of architects and engineers to be involved in the process of testing, and fee scales may have to be adjusted to allow for the extra time taken. The way the fee structure is set up in the UK doesn't encourage the degree of research necessary for invention. It is also equally important for client bodies to ensure that maintenance is carried out after the completion of building.

The benefits and rewards of innovation are often assessed in comparison with the potential risk and levels of investment required. However, it is difficult to establish who gains most from successful innovation, or who risks the greatest losses should an innovative solution fail. Every situation is likely to differ, depending on the contract, the liability and the strength of reputations. Clients gain from the status of association. Architects and engineers gain from their improved reputation. Manufacturers may gain most commercially if ideas are adapted as standard products.

A new language of technology is evolving as the construction process becomes increasingly complex. With the introduction of advanced materials into the construction realm we are no longer 'learning from Nellie' – the traditional method by which craftsmen's skills were acquired through an apprenticeship. Previously a dialogue of understanding existed between the different trades, with less onus on the architect to inform the parties of the construction sequence than is now necessary. Architects must ensure the communication of proper instruction to those responsible for the construction process and also ensure that they themselves gain knowledge of the manufacturing operations involved to enable an understanding of the limitations of the process. The following chapters are intended to describe the joy and the hardship in such a process.

Alan J. Brookes and Dominique Poole

Notes

1 M. Bowley (1960) *Innovations in building materials*, London: Gerald Duckworth & Co Ltd.

2 P. Rice (1994) *An engineer imagines*, London: Ellipsis.

3 M. Pawley (1987) 'Technology transfer', *Architectural Review*, no. 1087.

4 P. Buchanan (1993) *Renzo Piano building workshop complete works,* vol. 1, London: Phaidon Press.

5 A. Beukers (1998) *Lightness,* Rotterdam: 001 Publishers.

6 T. Robbin (1996) *Engineering a new architecture*, New Haven: Yale University Press.

7 E. De Maré (1948) *New ways of building*, London: The Architectural Press.

8 M. Cooley (1980) *Architect or bee? the human price of technology*, London: The Hogarth Press.

9 M. Pawley (1990) *Theory and design in the second machine age*, Oxford: Basil Blackwell Ltd.

10 J. Kaplicky and D. Nixon (1983) 'Skin: monocoque and semi-monocoque structures', *Architectural Review*, July.

11 G. Battle and C. McCarthy (1996) 'Multi-source synthesis: structural substance of composite detailing', *Architectural Design*, 66 (1/2).

12 A. J. Brookes (1999) 'Update on cladding', *The Architects' Journal*, 1 July, 210 (1).

13 A. J. Brookes (1998) 'Moulding architecture', *The Architects' Journal*, 10 Sept, 208 (9), pp.60–1.

14 I. McNeil (1996) *An encyclopaedia of the history of technology*, London: Routledge.

15 L. Rowell (1994) 'Tension in the roofscape', *AJ Focus*, July, 8 (7).

16 K. Wachsmann (1961) *The turning point of building, structure and design*, New York: Reinhold Publishing Corp.

17 B. Russell (1981) *Building systems, industrialization and architecture*, London: John Wiley & Sons.

Chapter 2

Exploring, rehearsing, delivering

Mike Davies, Richard Rogers Partnership

If you are innovating, you are dealing with new concepts, ideas and techniques. As an architect you are honour-bound to your client to understand the new and its implications, to do your homework and prepare as well as possible if you intend to question the rules and move architecture forward in some way. Where innovation in architecture occurs there is an implicit requirement for the architect to resort to experimentation, dedicated shepherding, continuous love and care, testing, mocking-up and going back again and again to get things right. Mock-ups are required in order to explain and demonstrate, to learn, refine, tune and to achieve the right overall assembly and performance.

The modern construction industry is now much more spiritually geared to what we at Richard Rogers Partnership (RRP) have been doing as a practice for the last thirty years, placing much more emphasis on manufacturing and prefabrication off the site, rather than on learning on the site. RRP are currently working on the Terminal 5 Project at London's Heathrow Airport, where the basic project design and construction philosophy includes extensive preconstruction development and making and testing mock-ups off site until everything is satisfactory and then assembly only on site. Conceptual and technical innovation is achieved in the factory except for smart erection improvements, which can only happen on site. Assembly on site only confirms the success of the process. Issues of site tolerances still remain but with maximum preconstruction there are vastly fewer major site decisions. This approach to projects contrasts with how architects and builders often worked in the 1960s and 1970s. The construction industry is definitely now less site experimental and more assembly orientated, although many projects of modest scale still don't have the time or resources available for extensive prototyping.

The construction industry is beginning to reflect other industries' skills better than before. It is beginning to be affected by the motor-car industry, the offshore oil industry and the information-management industry. It is also more universal and certainly pan-European, and these factors are conspiring to change the way we think about and design our buildings and about how we can build them more efficiently and effectively. This is certainly true for large-scale projects.

These new experimentation and fabrication attitudes, and also advanced computer-aided design (CAD) – a new creative weapon that cutting-edge designers are using very well – are together allowing the designer to invent, explore and create things that he or she could not countenance ten years ago.

2.1
Tribunal de Grande Instance, Bordeaux, France, 1992–8: a juxtaposition of ancient and modern showing the transparency of the building (architect: RRP)

2.2
The courtroom vessels took inspiration from oast houses and traditional boat building

2.3
The concave walls of the courtroom vessels have textural acoustic surfaces

Architects always had creative powers but didn't necessarily have the appropriate circumstances or the best tools with which to explore those powers. Now, advanced computing power allows the designer to really explore an idea while it is still an idea and to express that idea via the machine. Whereas before you painted a conceptual picture, now you can use advanced computing to illustrate, explore and describe the idea or concept in its evolution. The computer allows architects to describe complex shapes and geometries relatively easily, saving much time. Advanced CAD in the right creative hands is a real extension of the mind, the eye and the hand.

In the Bordeaux Law Courts project, completed in 1998, the RRP design team conceived a series of sculpturally complex onion-shaped courtrooms as a key functional but expressive element of the project. The design team moved from Ivan Harbour and Amo

Kalsi's beautiful hand sketches to a mathematically close equivalent, a trial-and-error process carried out on the computer until we arrived at a three-dimensional graphical and mathematical description which was generated by the machine but with which we were happy. This was then handed to the mainframe structure and interior finishes fabrication contractor, who understood the mathematical version of the shape and its constructional implications and who eventually fabricated the main timber frames and every wall panel inside these onion-shaped courtrooms perfectly, using that mathematical shape. No two panels are the same size; virtually every panel is customized – individual and different. We would never have been able to achieve or justify that approach in the 1970s; we would have had to standardize everything.

One of the ironies of the industry at the moment is that many big clients are standing out in the procurement firmament preaching, 'standardization, standardization', but actually have sometimes missed the boat and misunderstood the real opportunity. Technological improvement and change is accelerating and will leave Henry Ford standing still wondering where the world went. 'Custom' is now available because it is no more difficult to achieve than 'standard'. Multi-tasking production is the real secret; the new revolution. A new industrial production approach is happening in front of our eyes; multi-scaling, multi-tasking, off-site pre-assembly, just-in-time production, many different things coming off the same production machines – that is the real power emerging in the last two or three years. Computer-aided design has not only flourished as a creative tool for architects but has also come of age as a creative and flexible production tool. From the architect's eye to the finished product is now one process.

There are undoubtedly some benefits to standardization, to having more of the same, notably in prime costs, maintenance and repair, but there is little evidence that architectural quality is really improved by a slavish adherence to this philosophy, especially in a continually evolving user world. In my view, the ability to respond rapidly to new and evolving user demands will pre-empt the apparent benefits of the standard product. In the last five years the motor industry has forsaken Fordism.

RRP designed a little factory in Glasgow for Linn Products, who make top-of-the-range audio equipment. Our client was one of the first people in the country to pioneer multi-tasking assembly processes. One morning he would make speaker cabinets, the next morning toner arms, the next morning turntables, all in the same factory, on the same production line, with the same machines and the same people. In the Linn Products factory, robots bring table tops out of the store that are equipped for that day's task. At the end of the day the robots pick up the whole table, place it back in the store and collect the finished items. Then overnight the table is re-equipped with the tools and materials for the following day's task. There is a cry for standardization today, but what the cutting edge of the industry is now exploring is the exact negative of Henry Ford's production-line ethos of repetitive tasks day in day out.

RRP have been using a more time-effective way of constructing buildings for more than thirty years, with buildings constructed of kit parts. All the toilets for the Lloyd's Building were built in Bristol. The only thing that was done in London was to hoist the capsules into place, connect the supply and waste sockets and put in the soap. We use standard products and kit-construction approaches to enrich rather than regularize our designs. Today the industry pushes for standardization in order to achieve certainty and prediction, reliability and increased speed of construction – objectives we support and have argued for for many years. But for RRP standardization is just one of the means to the creative and individual end that we want to achieve: we are not afraid to resort to the 'custom', the

individual and 'original', to add magic where we judge that it moves the solution forward, especially if it is no more difficult or costly to achieve. There is also a perception of and a risk that standardization can relieve the architect of his or her individual responsibility and create boring catalogue architecture. The banishing of this risk all depends upon the talent and integrity of the hand to which you give the task. You have to rely on the creative powers of the good designer and his or her new tools to do more with less, with both standardization and customization as part of the total vocabulary. Architects such as John Nash and Giovanni Lorenzo Bernini produced beauty from standard components and from carefully selected custom interventions. In combination we can do no less.

I was a student at the Architectural Association in the late 1960s; my tutors were Fred Scott, David Green, Peter Cook and Ron Herron of Archigram. I originally came from the evening course at the Northern Polytechnic, where I and my fellows in the early 1960s had been blissfully unaware of the wider issues of architecture at large. It had a narrow teaching focus, concentrating on building regulations and actual building construction. We worked for

2.4
Lloyd's of London, 1978–86: the prefabricated lavatory pods, built in Bristol, were brought to the site on trucks and then hoisted into position prior to linking up to the service riser

2.5
Off-site mock-up of construction elements and materials, both internal and external, used to refine and perfect construction methodology prior to application on site

architects' offices during the day and went to architecture school in the evenings. The positive side of this was that I had built six small buildings and a substantial school science block before I arrived at the AA. I knew my construction; I literally detailed absolutely everything – every piece of steel and timber, every brick!

At the AA I met creative, bright colleagues in the most liberal, exploratory school of architecture on the planet at the time. I continued to develop my interest in innovative structures and became involved with lightweight and pneumatic structures. In my first year at the AA, along with four other bright students – Simon Conelly, Dave Harrison, David Martin and Johnny Devas – we researched, visited, fabricated and tested many lightweight structures. I also met up with Mark Fisher, another confirmed creative innovator, exploring the new.

In June 1968 the radical and far-sighted editor of *Architectural Design* magazine, Monica Pigeon, believed we had carried out significant research work and asked us to publish it. Our research became sixteen pages of *AD* and was entitled 'Pneu World'. It was the most definitive civilian overview of inflatable lightweight structures that has ever been produced. It very much reflected the spirit of the times at the AA, which was, for me, the era of the air-conditioned gypsy, the non-building, of doing things flexibly, avoiding building monuments, building more with less. The era focused on the individual, taking responsibility for his or her own environment. The key point was the aim of being autonomous. The paradigm was the snail; you didn't use any of the existing infrastructure, you'd take along your house and all of your survival gear and operate from there. From that notion stemmed a lot of interest in personal environments, from autonomous homes to the autonomous personal suit so eloquently championed by David Green of Archigram.

Whilst at the AA I also met Alan Stanton and Chris Dawson. On graduating we all obtained scholarships to the University of California in Los Angeles and promptly headed for the desert in California to try out our crazy inflatable structures, which we were building and experimenting with at the time. We were continuing a tradition that had begun at the AA in London, where as students we travelled around Europe, experimenting, as part of our college work. Our tutor, Ron Herron, defended us in a world where some tutors were saying, 'These students are just cruising Europe with lightweight structures and surviving by building, using and selling them – they are not in class and this isn't proper Architecture!' We had a fantastic time and learnt more in a month than at any other equivalent time in our lives about craftsmanship, process control, reliability, production speed, quick response, adaptation, human factors and autonomous living.

On joining Alan Stanton and Chris Dawson in the United States at UCLA we all formed a little design and art cabal called Chrysalis with three Americans (which name we subsequently sold to a well-known record company). We specialized in designing and building lightweight environments of one form or another, various structures – a mobile theatre, a mobile video van, an eco dome, various desert domes, a commercial product called pneu dome, an inflatable children's playpen, and many other odd structures – slightly nutty, interesting projects with lots of experimental feedback. In the spirit of *Dune*, the first eco-novel of the 1960s, we decided to build some oddball inflatable environments, some experimental solar collectors and desert survival suits for ourselves.

The desert suit was tested in the Palm Desert. We borrowed Darryl Zanuck's ranch, where the temperature out in the sun was about 185 degrees Fahrenheit. We obtained the obligatory roll of Mylar shiny film and cut out nice body-tailored outfits and silver drapes to keep the sun off. In the broiling heat, we put our silver suits on and were drenched to the skin within five seconds! We learnt very quickly that

in that environment, body transpiration is staggeringly high and without air circulation, you virtually drown in your own exuded body fluids! Back to the drawing board! – cookie cutters with spurs, prickly wheels all over the suits, vent holes! The modified suits were more tolerable – even though they were still sweaty, they were definitely keeping us cooler.

We had many experimental ideas and lots of feedback from our tests and practical trials. Were white inflatables cooler than dark inflatables? Why do the Tuareg dress in black? Airflow rate is critical! In one memorable erection of a Chrysalis autonomous air structure one of my colleagues dropped through the floor of our desert dome from 10 feet in the air just before it took to the skies in a strong wind! Foundations, good anchorage and spread stresses are even more critical in lightweight structures!

All these experiments gave us confidence and an understanding of construction and environmental engineering in the sense that, despite the fact that we were struggling with the boundaries, we were learning, imagining, creating and moving forward, achieving things. We built inflatable structures where the margin between comfort and discomfort is very slight; where small differences have big effects. If you watch an aircraft take off at Heathrow and look just above the wing on a damp day you see this flash of condensation vapour that comes and goes. It is remarkable to think that the vapour is forming and disappearing again in hundreds of millionths of a second. So these processes that we think are slow, like clouds, moisture and condensation, are actually happening at lightning speed with enormous energies associated with them. At one point, at 5.30 p.m. on a particular type of day in LA, all of a sudden the whole of the inside of one of our eco domes at Century City would become dripping wet – virtually instantly. Five minutes earlier the skin would be bone dry, then we would hit dew point and the walls would be running. Instant conversion from 'OK to oh no'! We spent a lot of time exploring these effects; if you increased air circulation through the structure you could stave off the transition for another hour or so. We learnt much about design and environmental engineering, not by conventional routes but by learning from practical experience, mock-ups, trial and error and experiment.

At the same time Steve Baer, from Albuquerque,

2.6
Chrysalis desert suits, 1960s

2.7
Steve Baer's house, Albuquerque, 1969

New Mexico, was designing and building his own house, which I consider to be the most important house of the 1960s – a very strong statement of eco principles of the time. The high desert around Albuquerque suffers from extremes of temperature, being very hot in the daytime and very cold at night. In 1969 Steve was building an adobe-walled house that had silver, aluminium-faced, 15-centimetre-thick insulative panels as external walls that hinged out and down. The whole house was designed to open and close by manual means. Every morning Steve would walk round and wind down his hinged walls to collect the sun and in the evening wind them up again to conserve the stored energy inside the house. The opening walls were reflective on the inside so that even more sun was reflected into the house when the walls were down. Behind the insulative walls was a glass skin and racks of oil drums filled with water and painted black. In the daytime the sun's heat was captured and stored in these oil drums, which raised the temperature of the water in the drums, acting as an energy buffer and keeping the house cool. At night the insulative walls were closed and the heat was re-radiated from the water-filled drums into the house as the external temperature dropped below freezing. The house was a perfect example of idealized natural principles. Steve had also installed a battery of solar-powered water heaters, a decent pumping windmill and an artesian well. He was as autonomous as you could get, living in harmony with the environment.

The spirit of the time was captured by a journal called *Whole Earth Catalog*. It represented and encapsulated an alternative lifestyle that was made viable by DIY, off-the-shelf things. Many young architects of the time were influenced by its philosophy but no big commercial architects or builders were using that approach. Large commercial buildings used additional energy purchased from the grid to cool them, which still seems insane in a part of the world where 0.7 of a kilowatt of free energy is falling on every square metre of ground surface. However, the innovations of the young experimenters of the 1960s have now come of age, manifested in the growth of eco concern and sustainability in modern contexts at the turn of the twenty-first century. Pressure is now being brought to bear on industry and commerce to innovate, to be smarter, to be more intelligent and do things responsibly.

I believe that RRP have managed to sustain a high level of architectural quality and integrity over many years. We maintain that level of architectural quality through rigour and cooperative work. Our most important design weapon is our collaborative power in terms of professional work. Many of the senior people in our relatively small practice have worked together for thirty years or so, which is probably unique. To get a dozen highly creative, completely differently skilled individuals to work together continually and constructively is not only an art in itself, but also a pleasure. A good practice needs a whole range of talents from creators to craftspeople.

A richness of intellect, of ideas and of creative and conceptual power there is aplenty, but RRP have also always recognized the value and contribution of skilled craftspeople in the practice who are good not only at dealing with the nitty-gritty real fabric of building but also at raising that fabric to a level of quality and vision that's well beyond the norm. To something that you do normally and of necessity, they bring real art and magic. They also follow right through to the end, including being in the factory monitoring each stage of the process. If you are innovating you need to deploy the full spectrum of talents, from originators to dedicated deliverers. If you are innovating you can't let go until the final nut and bolt are in place. You have to have concept-makers, movers, developers, doers, providers, polishers and finishers. RRP have a multi-disciplinary team who all have different talents and qualities but

2.8
IRCAM: the Institute for Research and Coordination in Acoustics and Music at the Centre Pompidou, Paris, France 1971–7 (architect: RRP)

2.9
Inmos Microprocessor Factory, Newport, South Wales, 1982: the clean room (architect: RRP)

who are all drawn by the new concepts, the rigour of their development, by new processes, new materials and new approaches as a means for moving architecture forward. Above all, we respect each other's different talents. In combination, we are a very strong and robust team.

Most of the interesting architectural firms are very lateral. RRP are looking outside architecture all the time. I am as interested in wind farms, solar energy, telescopes, dams and hydroelectric projects, in art, electronics and new fabrics, as I am in architecture, engineering and construction. The whole time one is looking for improved performance or ingenious ways of doing what nature does so well. Nature programmes are interesting for us – they are a huge resource of concepts and ideas contributing to the next building. Nature is still a direct and valuable analogue for us in parallel with all the other criteria and parameters that result in a good design and a good building of integrity. I remember asking Pierre Boulez, the composer and client for the Institute for Research and Coordination in Acoustics and Music (IRCAM) at the Centre Pompidou, what

were the most important criteria in his musical compositions. Boulez said, 'The most important things about my composition are the overall concept of the piece and its rigour and discipline; how do you decide to start, and how do you decide you have finished? Everything in between is simple!' I thought, how absolutely right; how do you create a clear, conceptual, driving idea that inherently carries the discipline and guidance for the doing and how do you decide when to stop?

At the time of the Centre Pompidou my personal responsibility within the practice was IRCAM. Among his demands for the research centre, Boulez, an absolute perfectionist, wanted a huge studio that was the most extreme in the world – acoustically modifiable by three different mechanisms all at once. There is no studio anywhere else in the world where this is possible. Boulez and his team wanted to modify sound not only electronically, by time delay, and acoustically, by change of absorptive texture within the given fixed volume, but also by modifying the total volume and shape of the studio at will! A tall order by any measure. All the walls and all the ceilings have completely changeable surfaces and the resulting volume of the main studio room can vary by a colossal 400 per cent, with height variations of 15 metres within the volume. We can alter the characteristics of the space to simulate the conditions of other great concert halls of the world. The solution that we came up with was highly innovative, technologically complex and required substantial acoustic experimentation and innovation driven by new and specific state-of-the-art requirements.

Many of the projects that I and the practice as a whole have been involved with have been focused on the front end of the industry or the front end of technology. Inmos, the government microprocessor factory in Newport, was unique in that nobody had built a huge, highly flexible, class 'O' clean room to the required scale and standard in the UK at the time.

The day-to-day client, Bob Holmstrom from Oregon, who worked closely with RRP here in the UK, was extraordinarily catalytic in his technological overview and wanted a building that would last for seven years! In Holmstrom's experience in the microchip industry in the USA, after seven years microchip production technology would have changed so much that the building itself would be redundant! RRP took a different approach: questioning the industry standards, turning things on their heads, developing new concepts, building mock-ups and prototypes of key high-performance elements, we utilized kit construction to the maximum and designed a highly adaptable, highly modularized, loose-fit but very high-performance building. Successive computer companies have bought the building and continued microchip production with new processes, proving that it was truly flexible and is still a highly adaptable and highly productive building now, twenty years later.

A robust concept with inherent flexibility was the key to success. Even the concept of the façade was robust enough to survive client change. It used an inside-out patent glazing system with changeable panels, deliberately informal and locally flexible, allowing the client to exchange glass panels, solid panels, grilles, doors and access panels at will – a concept based on everyday client needs rather than formal purity, utility rather than an untouchable set piece. There is an arts analogy here: pre-1964, sculpture in the UK was on pedestals – you looked at it, you didn't touch it, it was form on formal display. The 'New Generation' exhibition at the Whitechapel Gallery changed all that in 1965. The sculptures exhibited were all on the ground – no pedestals in sight! – a revolution. This marked the progression from hallowed object to utilitarian object, from sculpture on the pedestal to sculpture on the ground – colourful, touchable, sittable on, utilitarian, more connected, more accessible, more informal, free. The same concepts were appearing in architecture, in cinema, in painting and in poetry. *Beyond the gentility principle*, Alfred Alvarez' great 1960s' poetry critique, blew formal poetry aside, creating new space for the poetry of our time. In the cinema, *Saturday Night and Sunday Morning*, the cinema of everyday life, placed *Gone with the Wind* and John Wayne on the shelf. From formal icons to the poetry of the everyday. Architecture is undergoing the same change in the UK.

Change is all about us. There is an enormous revolution happening right now – especially with regard to the effects of the computer. As a result of CAD, many young architects can't draw by hand very well anymore; we now have people who have double first degrees and who are fantastically bright but can't spell to save their lives. My generation, who read for entertainment rather than watching the TV, didn't have this problem. Some young architects are highly articulate but stumped without the machine. Aware of this, in our practice we try to merge the two skills; we try to draw as much as we use the machine as a tool. Concepts are not created by the machine; the concept is still from the mind but we use the machine to develop and convey it, sometimes achieving the previously unaffordable and occasionally the impossible.

I believe that architectural morality is changing as a result of the machine's ability to evoke things that you can't build and to explore and express ideas that were not possible to demonstrate easily before. I believe that technology and art are really coming together for the first time in many years. If the 1960s and early 1970s were technologically bullish and optimistic, then the late 1970s and 1980s were outstandingly exploratory but uncertain technologically. Now, in the last decade, with the new weaponry of the computer, we have the ability to deal with the concept, the fabric, the form, the technology, the art and the spirit of things. Now the computer sometimes allows us to capture this spirit in ways that we couldn't illustrate before and render it in detail to levels of perfection that still astonish!

Today, architecture is evolving, partly because of the magic of our tools.

For me, much is still to do with experimentation. The most interesting practices are those taking on the odder challenge, the difficult brief, the new problem. As a result, they are obliged to look at new things in unusual ways and are informed by these odd things and ways. If you take on a challenge you stretch yourself. Architects stretch themselves with the new materials of their time. They are being more inventive with structure, with skin, with materials, with glass façades, and they are trying to be more economical by using less energy in our buildings via greater holistic thinking. Nevertheless, I don't believe a holistic archetype of an eco building for the twenty-first century has yet been built. In the UK there are pieces of good energy-efficient architecture emerging. Energy innovation is now all around us. But I fear that the driving ideas of sustainability will be less powerful in six or seven years. There is a certain amount of fashion associated with sustainability at the moment and sustainability is now used like salt and pepper on every project you see. Buildings with solar façades are pushing forward, raising questions, but the really smart buildings are still to come.

One of my favourite buildings is the great solar furnace building in the south of France, at Odeillo, a twelve-storey research centre on a mountain slope. On the south façade there are ten floors of orthodox research labs and offices; on the north side, the biggest solar furnace on the planet. An enormous parabolic segmented mirror, itself fed by a hillside full of sun-tracking mirrors, focuses sunlight into an incredible central furnace tower. The Odeillo solar furnace is a wonderful mixed-technology, mixed-use building. On one side of the tower, office desk-work; on the other, a 6000-degrees-Fahrenheit focal point from which steel pours like rain. For me office work, research and dramatic experimentation are combined into one of the most extraordinary mixed-use buildings that exists.

2.10 (previous page)
Kitt Peak McMath Solar Telescope in Arizona (architect: Skidmore, Owings and Merrill)

I am increasingly suspicious of buildings dedicated to a specific use. We should be building many more experimental multi-use buildings, challenging the norm, redefining use, lifestyle and operation.

Another of my favourite buildings is a Skidmore, Owings, & Merrill building, the Kitt Peak McMath Solar Telescope in Arizona, which has a thermally controlled environment for the biggest solar telescope on the planet. Beautiful architecturally and stunningly detailed, the façade of the building is a water-cooled copper skin. The inside is kept at an absolutely constant temperature to within half a degree by variable flow of the water through the skin. The façade is dynamically responsive. Back to nature with technological precision and beauty.

I have been fascinated over many years with the idea of responsive skins and the notion of buildings with mechanical and electrical and environmental systems that are integral with the façade rather than inside the building. If you organize your buildings and façades correctly you don't need all the radiators and subsystems inside, you merely transfer energy around the skin to combat extreme conditions. The idea of responsive buildings that are intelligent enough to monitor themselves and to monitor and respond to external conditions seems common sense and good economics to me. You call on self-powered, dynamic, electro-chemical systems embedded within the skin of the building to modulate incoming energy as necessary rather than purchasing extra energy to combat the job nature and the environment intended – certainly a more sustainable and lower-energy building concept and absolutely an integral part of the skin and bones of the building. I have been working on dynamic skins for thirty years and RRP have played a significant part in persuading the glazing industry to explore variable skin concepts. We are only a few years away from the fully solid-state, variable-property, self-powered façade.

I think that manufacturers' and designers' attitudes are being changed by new production processes. In the Millennium Dome we designed a large number of steel-framed staircases. The way to fabricate most effectively was to make them out of an enormously thick plate, cutting odd shapes out, just like pieces of a jigsaw puzzle. The steel industry is now capable of doing this because we can now cut steel in free-form shapes of enormous thickness and of considerable complexity using computer-controlled cutting with a water jet. The actual shape becomes irrelevant.

Many building industry firms have been revolutionized by changes in their processes. The contractor providing the steelwork for Heathrow Terminal 5 has now installed the most sophisticated steel production and handling facility in Europe at present. It is an extremely advanced, fully computerized production line, with capabilities completely different from the orthodox 'standardized' approach. The computer-controlled cutting, handling and welding machines are able to fabricate things you would not otherwise be able to make, in many ways that were not possible until now. This is a formidable advantage in the production and construction of Terminal 5, given its huge scale.

The subcontractors, now framework partners with BAA, have particular qualities of innovation and production within their organizations. They tend to be the leading contractors in the industry; excelling themselves in one way or another, and have been picked out because they are ahead of the game. They have invested in clever kit, clever people, and generally are in the forefront of pan-European industry. We tend to gravitate towards people who themselves are seen to be exploring and innovating. Certainly one of the things we enjoy as a practice is the ability to see the next step. We like to see the boundaries being pushed a little. We like to work with contractors, partners and clients who question the norm and who are open and contribute to new ideas and methodologies.

The knowledge and exploration network amongst

architects is quite powerful. I have a great respect for some architectural contemporaries – people whose technical integrity I know I can trust. I know that there are people in other good firms who are very talented and who are also trying to innovate, whether it be in urban and planning terms or in the design response or fabric of buildings. There are inter-practice jungle tom-toms, information flow and a certain competitive edge between peer architects, but it is not as competitive as people generally perceive. Our practice would far prefer to lose a competition to Norman Foster's or Renzo Piano's practices than to some dreadful second-rate hack. There is a lot of constructive and creative talking between different practices and also a rich dialogue with the industry – all of which stimulates innovation, synthesis and new design and construction.

If 50 per cent of what RRP do is creative in the traditional architectural design sense, then 50 per cent is creative in all sorts of ways that are not directly to do with building design per se, such as persuading the client, dealing with the local authority, dealing with English Heritage, cost, time and so on. None of these support activities is the primal creative act but they are all ways of defending the concept, the idea, paradigm or process against erosion, as most of the support processes tend to conspire to erode the original concept. We need ideas, new methodologies and innovation right across the board, not just in the fabric design and technology of buildings. We need very straightforward goals to keep the concepts and processes clear.

The design team at the Millennium Dome spent an enormous amount of time making the structure as light as possible. There were three or four significant steps in the gradual development of the concepts where innovation in structural terms was fundamental. The original iteration was my sketch for a 380-metre-diameter dome suspended from a ring of columns. Then we got cold feet about the enormous spans; Buro Happold and ourselves

thought that we would never hold it up and a second supporting line of columns was proposed. After looking at that, we thought it was also too complex. Ian Liddell, our engineer, refined the concept further, proposing a ring of flying struts to help the span – still not right. We then increased the diameter of the earlier ring of columns and eliminated all others, effectively moving back towards the original concept. At a memorable directors' design meeting at which the whole team was present, we recognized that, despite refinements, they were still too close together. The whole design team opted for greater flexibility and a more dynamic and aesthetically better-proportioned design with the columns further apart. We arrived at the final design by using less and less material and making the dome lighter and lighter. The whole dome weighs about the same as a cube of water 12 metres high. The fire strategy took months of sheer hard labour to develop; the solution was quite obvious, but to persuade the various parties and authorities to adopt that solution took a lot of time.

Our practice is about a whole series of attributes and interests, exploratory things – partly science, partly art, partly human and social ideas, partly a group gut feeling. I believe that our group judgement is almost unassailable and by the time an idea has satisfied the scrutiny and all the particular concerns of the dozen design directors then that idea has sufficient integrity to survive most tests – which is why RRP can deliver such unorthodox but nevertheless appropriate buildings within tough contractual time and cost contexts.

Most innovation and much of the best design stems from being more questioning, more honest, more economical with material, more direct in response and, as a result, creating a more challenging, uplifting and magical solution. Invention and innovation are a key part of our lives and it is through this that we contribute to architecture, urbanism and society at large.

Chapter 3

Concept before calculation

Tony Hunt, Tony Hunt Associates Ltd

I draw because I want to see.
  Carlo Scarpa, Sergio Los, Taschen 1999. p. 10.

Drawing has always been my way of seeing my idea of a design – a mixture of orthogonal and axonometric – always thinking about the way that the parts of things are joined together. Different materials have different constraints and their methods of connection require quite difference approaches.

I was brought up on Meccano, making many small plastic models, and then became fascinated by powered model aircraft, designing my own whilst still at school. It was my father who 'knew someone in the city' who offered me a job in his small consulting engineering practice. I was taken on as an articled pupil and learnt the basics while studying part-time but there was no inspiration in that firm and, having become interested in all aspects of design and particularly architecture, I nearly changed course.

The Festival of Britain was a turning point. It opened my eyes to what was exciting in the world of engineering and architecture. The two most powerful exhibits for me were the Dome of Discovery – which I still believe is an important structure – and the Skylon – even more important and innovative, with its tensegrity-type supports. Suddenly engineering was wonderful and I was fortunate to get a job with

Felix Samuely, the engineer of the Skylon, who, like Ove Arup, was a man who understood architects and worked alongside them as a creative designer – a very unusual type of engineer in the 1950s. Samuely's structures were inventive and innovative and he was expert in building with steel, concrete and timber, sometimes in unusual combinations. I spent seven very formative years with the firm, first with 'Sammy', as he was called, and, after he died, with Frank Newby and Sven Rindl, who was head of our studio.

It was at this time that, through Frank Newby, I got to know about the work of Konrad Wachsmann, Charles Eames and others and, through my first wife, Pat, who worked at the Arts Council, developed an

(Clockwise from left)

3.1
Control line model aircraft designed and built by Tony Hunt at age fifteen, while at school

3.2
The Skylon, Festival of Britain, 1951, designed by Felix Samuely with Powell and Moya

3.3
Konrad Wachsmann, joint details

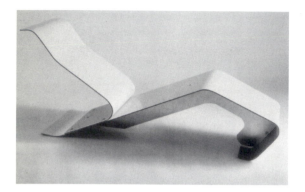

3.4
Chaise longue in alucobond, designed by Tony Hunt for Aram Designs, 1987

3.5
The 'Retreat', an adjunct to Creek Vean House, Cornwall, with Team 4, 1964–6

interest in sculpture and painting. One of my other passions was, and is, furniture and a successful entry in an Italian Cantú competition led me to make a change and go to work for Terence Conran as a furniture and exhibition designer. This was in 1959, at a time when the design team consisted of only three people plus the directors. My tenure didn't last, owing to a personality clash, and I joined a small firm of architects, Morton Lupton, where I spent two years as their engineer in house. They also had a furniture design and manufacturing business and, as well as designing structures for the practice, I designed a range of furniture, which was put into the ML furniture catalogue.

The architectural practice of Morton Lupton was dissolved and I left to set up on my own with the help of Frank Newby, who enabled me to get my practice up and running. At this time (1962) a number of young architects, some of whom I already knew, were setting up on their own and I started working with them on quite large projects both for private clients and universities. My technological opportunity came through an introduction to Team 4 from Wendy Foster, whom I had met when she was working with architect Paul Manousso.

My collaboration with Team 4 started in Cornwall with the Retreat and Creek Vean House, followed by several other small housing schemes. Soon after this I had the chance, also with Team 4, to put into practice some of my ideas about simple, elegant, repetitive steel structures. The Reliance Controls

building was just that. Probably the first of its kind, it was a single-storey industrial building with just four main structural elements: column with cross-head, main beam, secondary beam and diagonal bracing. It was designed for repetition in future phases, was welded on site and was incredibly simple. The roof and wall cladding, both in profile metal sheet, were designed as spanning structures acting as diaphragms. It was difficult even at this early stage of my practice to know who designed what. It was a complete synthesis of architecture, structure and services and was, for me, the beginnings of an ambition to work closely with other designers to achieve the collaboration that now occurs amongst so many design groups.

This is just one strand of my work, which has developed through my office and has resulted in a number of significant structures with different architects. It was at this time that I was invited by Sir Hugh and Lady Casson to spend a day a week teaching what was then an interior design course at the Royal College of Art, where most of the students were actually doing architecture. This led to my writing a basic Structures Notebook as a simple non-mathematical guide, which has subsequently been published. Students tend to remember their tutors and many years later I find myself working with three of them – James Dyson, Jon Wealleans and John Furneaux. Teaching to me is an important strand of my work: it informs the students and at the same time is a challenge to the teacher to communicate structural knowledge and ideas, building knowledge for both parties.

The philosophy behind the Reliance Controls building led to, among other things, two steel-frame houses with Richard and Su Rogers, who by now had set up on their own, and then, also with them, a perfume factory and office for Universal Oil Products, a French company setting up in England. Here we again developed a simple, repetitive steel frame, this time with lattice primary girders and again using only three structural elements combined with a glass-reinforced concrete (GRC) cladding panel system. A building for IBM at Portsmouth followed with what was by now Foster Associates. Here again there was absolute simplicity of structure – one column type and two lattice girder types resulting from a performance specification written by myself and designed to be simply extended. In this building the whole of the perimeter was clad in a simple floor-to-roof Astrawall glazing system.

While this was going on and the office was expanding we were involved in three major projects in reinforced concrete: Alexandra Road Housing with Neave Brown at Camden, Newport High School with Eldred Evans and Davide Shalev and Leicester Library with Christopher Dean of Castle and Park, with whom I had worked earlier on a hall of residence, also for Leicester University. Technology

occurred in these buildings in different ways. Alexandra Road was a huge scheme and we originally designed it totally in precast concrete. It was subsequently changed to largely *in-situ* casting at the request of the contractors – the wrong decision as it turned out. Newport High School, the result of a competition we had entered with six different architects, consisted largely of long shallow spans in *in-situ* concrete, supporting one-way, deep-trough concrete units. The library at Leicester University was an exercise in creating an air-conditioned building while keeping within the strict cost limits of what was then the University Grants Committee. It consisted of hollow structural columns and beams feeding air to hollow floor units from a rooftop plant room, eliminating all metal ductwork. The design was developed into the patented Structair system. One of the other entries for the Newport High School competition, by Foster Associates, was influenced by the SCSD (School Construction System Development) programme, which had been developed by Ezra Ehrenkrantz and his team in California. The building for IBM was also influenced by this system.

An important and dramatic concrete structure followed on from this, which was, of course, the headquarters for Willis Faber & Dumas in Ipswich with Foster Associates. A steel frame was conceived originally but the nature of the architecture, together with fire regulations, led us to consider fair-faced

3.6
Rogers' House, Wimbledon, with Richard and Su Rogers, 1968

3.7
Willis Faber & Dumas, Ipswich, with Foster Associates, 1971–5

The 'shed' evolved via a series of design and model studies. It was initially conceived as a series of giant portal frames spanning 35 metres, with alternatives for cladding outside or inside the frame. This truly monumental portal scheme was, one momentous Thursday, scrapped by Norman, saying over coffee 'I'm sorry Tony. I'm not happy with the structure. We need to rethink it from scratch whilst retaining the overall concept of the all-enveloping volume.' Back to the drawing board at a very late stage. The main structure had already been priced and we thought it was going ahead.

3.8
The Sainsbury Centre, Norwich, with Foster Associates, 1974–8

concrete. The structure was in effect 'frameless'. By using a deep, two-way, waffle floor with solid infill at the column heads the use of down-stand beams was avoided, even on a 14 x 14-metre grid, with the floors around the perimeter and escalator well cantilevering 3 metres. The building is best known, of course, for its all-enveloping perimeter glass wall, which hangs from the roof slab falling the full three storeys to avoid differential movement problems at the cantilevered floor-slab edges. The glazing design was a close collaboration between architect, engineer, cladding consultant – Martin Francis – and manufacturer. It was the first of its kind and led to the development of sophisticated frameless glazing systems.

But back to steel, with Fosters again. Sir Robert Sainsbury was intending to donate his fabulous art collection to the University of East Anglia. The building to house this was to be combined with facilities for the university, including a research library, senior common room and restaurant, and was to be called the Sainsbury Centre. It was clear to me from early on that, despite other alternatives being explored for the building, what Norman Foster really wanted was a clear-span dramatic building in complete contrast to the campus that Denys Lasdun had created. Here was a client brief for a building on a virgin site with few constraints – always more difficult than a tight set of conditions.

Time was by now short. We explored the possibility of using the aluminium triodetic system but all the know-how for this system was based in Canada and the development time necessary would have jeopardized the programme. So we embarked on the solution that was built. This comprised a series of identical steel-lattice tower columns supporting prismatic lattice girders. All towers and girders are identical except for those at each end of the building, where pairs of columns and girders are linked via scissor bracing to provide a wind frame. The towers and girders were of identical depth (2.4 metres) to make a 'match' and to provide for servant spaces in both the wall and roof zones.

A key detail is the external junction between column and girder structure, which was to have a curved cladding panel that was in conflict with the angular corner of the structure. I remember well the design team drawing the structure full size while lying on the floor at Norman's house in the country and resolving the problem in the same way one would in the furniture, exhibition and boat industries – called 'lofting'.

The Sainsbury Centre ended up as one of the most satisfying projects and it is still one of my favourites. Although not the lightest structure, it has great clarity and is an excellent example of architecture, structure and services coming together to create a great building.

3.9

Mock-up of aluminium-frame house, Hampstead, for Norman and Wendy Foster, 1978–9

3.10

British Antarctic Survey Base, Halley Bay, with Angus Jamieson, 1983

3.11

Detail of Patera System, with Michael Hopkins, 1983

During the construction of the Sainsbury Centre I bought a large house in the Cotswolds and opened a second office there. Some significant work from that period includes a house for Norman and Wendy Foster, designed initially with a steel frame and subsequently with an aluminium frame, based on ideas from aircraft technology. Celia Williams from the office and I worked intensively on this project with Norman and Wendy, Richard Horden and Tony Pritchard. We built full-size prototypes of both structures, erected in the grounds of Norman's country house, but the project was in the end abandoned.

Two fascinating but completely different projects then appeared. Structaply, a manufacturer of timber buildings, approached us via the architect Angus Jamieson to design a timber replacement for the failing metal structure at Halley Bay in the Antarctic for the British Antarctic Survey. Working with Mark Whitby, who was working in our office at that time,

we devised an interlocking system of double-skinned, curved, insulated plywood panels that were all identical and interlocked to form 9-metre-diameter tubes, designed to be progressively buried beneath the snow at a rate of 1 metre per year. Inside these tubes were a series of two-storey timber buildings housing all the base's activities. A prototype was built and I remember well having a celebratory dinner in it before it was dismantled to become part of the whole shipment – a bit like the dinner that Brunel had in the Thames Tunnel! The whole kit was shipped out after another party on board just before sailing. The tubes were constructed in a trench cut in the snow, temporarily propped and then backfilled with snow. The design life was relatively short since the snow, which acted rather like a fluid, built up year by year until, finally, the tubes started distorting rather in the manner of the previous construction in Armco, but lasting for a longer period.

The second project was for a client who approached Michael Hopkins wanting a prefabricated building system that could be used for a number of different purposes and which he intended to build by setting up a dedicated manufacturing plant. The original idea was to develop an aluminium system that we had been working on with Michael's office, with input from Ian Ritchie. We were having problems with the jointing of the elements and asked the client if we could start from scratch. He agreed and we, with Mark Whitby again, developed the

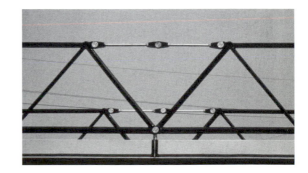

3.12
Inmos Microprocessor Factory, Newport, South Wales, with Richard Rogers Partnership, 1982

3.13
Detail of Inmos Microprocessor Factory

Patera System. It basically consisted of one lattice column type, one lattice beam with a 'clever' joint and a double-skinned, steel cladding panel that was used for both walls and roof. Junctions between panels were made with a specially developed neoprene gasket. Two prototypes were built at Stoke-on-Trent and subsequently re-erected at Canary Wharf. The system design was scaled up for a number of different configurations, one of which was used for the Hopkins office in Broadley Terrace. Sadly, the client decided not to proceed with the project and, like so many good ideas in industrialized building, it was never put into production.

It was around this time that Inmos Microelectronics approached Richard Rogers Partnership to design a plant for a new company with very advanced ideas in microchip design and manufacture. I had already worked with the client, Iann Barron, some years ago on the Computer Technology facility at Hemel Hempstead. There the architect had been Foster Associates, but this time he decided to go to the 'other' high tech architect of the time. I was at a meeting in Rogers' office on another project and after lunch was asked to join a

further meeting. This was when Inmos was in its early stages. I asked why I was there and either Richard or Mike Davies said: 'Oh, didn't we tell you? We've recommended you as engineers for the project so we would like your views!' The job became a fascinating exercise in devising a giant Meccano-type kit capable of simple linear extension at a future date. David Hemmings, who had been the chief designer on Willis Faber & Dumas, ran the job with Allan Bernau and Alan Jones.

The original site for Inmos was just outside Bristol in a wonderful prominent spot but after the preliminary design had been completed the politics of the Thatcher government dictated that it should go to South Wales. We picked the whole design up and moved it 50 or so miles west to Newport but had to completely redesign the foundation system for what, in geotechnical terms, was a difficult site.

The structure incorporated a number of innovations. It was completely exoskeletal as structure-free interior spaces were a client requirement. Hence it became a design exercise in producing a coherent, repetitive, external structure that not only supported the roof and wall cladding

3.14
Schlumberger Research, Cambridge, with Michael Hopkins & Partners, 1985

but also provided a multi-storey central platform for all the complex services units – another client requirement allowing ease of changeability and servicing in a building that was to be in non-stop use. Our aim for the structure was to have the maximum size parts fabricated in the works with maximum repetition, not only of main elements but also of joints, many of which were steel castings. Our concept of using stainless-steel shear pins as connections was incorporated in virtually all the site joints and, with one exception (at the root of the main trusses), used a single pin. Thus the structure was truly pin-jointed. The benefits of this approach were seen in the incredible speed of erection of the frame.

Continuing in the high tech theme, we were invited by Michael Hopkins to work with him on a building for Schlumberger Research in Cambridge. Since the 1950s, when collaboration between architect and engineer was becoming more common, certain structural 'preoccupations' have come to the fore at certain times. Examples such as thin concrete shells, timber hyperbolic paraboloids, steel space frames and other structural types came to prominence and were then superseded in popularity by some 'new' structural form. Tension-assisted masted structures became one of these. Inmos was one of the earliest of the tension-assisted steel structures, along with the Cummins Engine building at Quimper, France, engineered by Peter Rice. Schlumberger followed on from these in a most dramatic way. The commission was for a building to house a new research facility for oil-well drilling and included a test station, laboratories and offices.

Once the basic form and management of the buildings had been agreed, I came up with alternative roof types based on compression vault-like structures. Meanwhile, Michael Hopkins was getting hooked on tensile membranes. The outcome was, of course, an exoskeletal structure both for office and laboratory buildings and for the system suspending the membranes over the three main spaces.

Resolution of the geometry of the main structure was complex, including, as it must, a system whereby the whole aerial structure and supporting masts would remain in place if the membrane roof had to be replaced for any reason. Despite my misgivings at one point, the whole structure came together well notwithstanding its complexities. One of the main problems came about during erection of the masts and tension rods. The structural assembly was very sensitive and any one adjustment affected the positions of other points in space. Thus it was a case of multiple small adjustments until all the mast ends were in the correct position before erection of the main membrane roof cables.

Membrane roofs became something of an obsession for me. Few firms of engineers had any knowledge of their special design complexities, which had been developed by Frei Otto at the Institute of Lightweight Structures in Stuttgart, and continued by Ted Happold and his office. The opportunity for such a roof came with a large project in Brighton for a roof over a multi-purpose theme park. Our investigations were developed with Peter Heppel, who had become expert through research into the aerodynamics of yacht sails – a parallel technology. This project, sadly, was abandoned by the client but we learnt a lot about form-finding via models, fabric behaviour and cutting patterns. Following the Brighton project we were involved with a number of small tensile membrane structures, one at Alton Towers, some at Glasgow Garden Festival and a group of four membrane-roofed temporary buildings that ended up as the factory for Landrell, themselves membrane fabricators.

Don Valley Athletics Stadium, which we won in competition with other engineers, seemed an ideal vehicle for exploring the use of a membrane roof on a large scale. There was no requirement for insulation but it would be advantageous to have filtered light through the roof – a tensile membrane was ideal. The resulting roof structure in PTFE (polytetrafluoroethylene) was a combination of forms, using arches and cones, curved cable boundaries and straight edges. At the time (1991) it was the largest PTFE membrane roof in the UK.

In 1989, BAA announced a competition for a fifth terminal at Heathrow Airport and we, with Yorke, Rosenberg, Mardall architects, entered. The scale of the project was enormous and what fascinated me was the opportunity to create an airport terminal with dramatically large spans. We devised a series of vaulted roofs based on a central span of 144 metres for the main hall, with roofs over the side halls spanning 72 metres. The main girders for these roofs were steel prismatics at 36-metre intervals supported on giant concrete columns. These girders were to be clad, probably in Teflon glass fabric, to provide the flow and return air ducts. Spanning between the main girders was a double curved steel diagrid that was post tensioned by internal struts and clad in translucent double glazing. Sadly our team didn't win

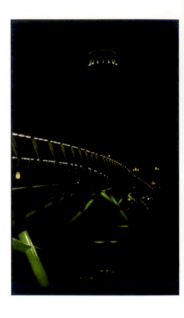

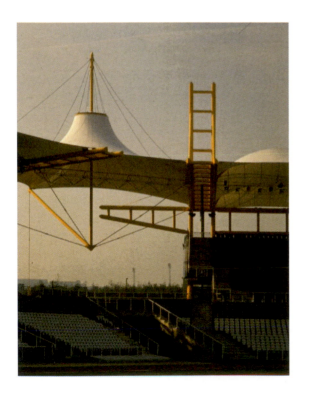

– a great regret to me, as one of my passions is devising structures to cover large, clear spaces with the minimum of internal support. From the technical point of view, designing on such a large scale would have been a little daunting but at the same time a wonderful challenge.

The next interesting challenge came with another competition, this time for the Acropolis Museum in Athens. Sitting in a café on one of the designated sites with my wife, Jan Kaplicky and Amanda Levete, we devised ideas for the basic plan and section of our building, which I, with Nick Green, developed into a clear-span roof (again!). This was to be a diagrid made up of aluminium vierendeel girders spanning onto a perimeter concrete ellipse, with lightweight, steel-structured internal floors. The pedestrian bridge that spanned the main road between the museum and the Acropolis was a long-span, stressed ribbon bridge using cables and a deck made up of interlocking precast concrete units. But we faced failure again as this scheme was not even accepted for the second stage.

Also with Jan and Amanda of Future Systems, we entered a competition for a pedestrian bridge

3.16
West India Quay Bridge, London Docklands, with Future Systems, 1994

3.17
West India Quay Bridge, London Docklands

3.15
Don Valley Athletics Stadium, Sheffield, with Sheffield City Architects, 1991

3.18
Waterloo International Terminal, London, with Nicholas Grimshaw & Partners, 1993

across West India Dock. This time we won with the simple concept of a floating pontoon bridge. The idea, proposed by Jan and tweaked by me, was agreed at our first meeting. The design was, of course, modified as design development took place but the basic principle never changed from day one – pontoons supporting X-form tubular struts, in turn supporting a central spine. Outriggers from this spine carry an extruded aluminium deck.

The beginning of the Waterloo International Terminal Project was extraordinary. I was telephoned one morning by Michael Edwards, an architect with British Rail. He asked me to meet him at Waterloo Station to look at a model of a proposed new international terminal. The model had a multitude of masts and cables and was painted pink. On being asked, I said that I thought it was too complex and also probably unstable. To my surprise I was then asked if I would be interested in carrying out a feasibility study, with costs, for a new train-shed. I worked with Neil Thomas, (now Atelier One), and we produced a number of studies – six, I think – which were narrowed down for presentation. Soon after this, British Rail decided to go outside their

architectural department to find an independent firm. A number were considered and the job went to Nicholas Grimshaw & Partners, with us retained as structural engineers.

The brief was then reappraised from scratch and went through a number of alterations before the solution you see today. From our point of view there were a number of critical constraints. The site boundaries, which curved and tapered, were fixed, as were the track alignments. The maximum height of the roof was determined by a proposed 'air rights' building, designed by others and abandoned after a public outcry but too late for us to change our cross-section geometry. This, coupled with the lack of a platform on the west side of the station, resulted in an asymmetric cross-section. To achieve this, Alan Jones, the design director, and Grimshaws cleverly positioned the upper pin of the three-pin arch off-centre, enabling the upper and lower members of the main trusses to use their compression and tension forces according to the way the arch behaved.

One design decision that was followed through vigorously was the use of steel castings for all the major joints. There was an enormous amount of repetition, which meant casting was very economical. The main trusses vary in span from 45 metres to 38 metres because of the site shape and again, to be economical, we devised sets of compression tubes, reducing in diameter according to load, with lengths based on the longest span trusses and the same tube sizes in shorter lengths used for the shorter spans.

The other real challenge was in the various glazing systems. The west wall, for instance, had to be capable of vertical, horizontal and racking movement since a train entering the station causes a deflection 'wave' in the concrete main support structure. This, coupled with the varying plan geometry, resulted in some complex but again repetitive design solutions using adjustable stainless-steel brackets and both sliding and concertina joints

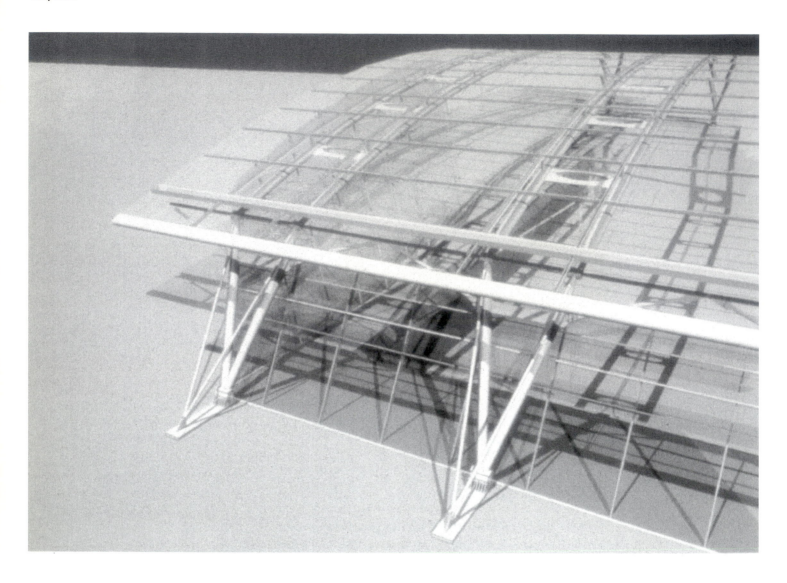

in neoprene. The glazing of the concourse wall is probably one of the lightest yet conceived, with slender mast-like mullions braced by cold-drawn stainless-steel rods and stainless-steel castings.

In 1997, through Wolf Mangelsdorf, a young German engineer in our office, we were invited by Petra Wörner of Wörner and Partners in Frankfurt to join them in the third and final stage of a competition for Stuttgart 21 – a proposed station for the high-speed German ICE train network. The jury had suggested that the architects should find a 'more imaginative' firm of engineers to help them to progress their design.

This was, for me, an amazing project – long spans (95 metres clear) and another international railway station. Wolf and I, working both here and in the architect's office, developed, after some trial ideas, a prestressed, primary arch, roof-truss system with asymmetrical supports. These supports were influenced by the differing conditions at each end.

3.19
Stuttgart 21 Station, with Wörner and Partners, 1997

There were, of course, other major parts to the proposed station but our inventiveness went into the train-shed roof. It was totally glazed and for ventilation had giant sliding roof panels that followed the contours of the convex outer curve of the main trusses. We convinced the stringent local proof engineers that we had a viable and buildable solution, which was presented at a formidable meeting to the client, Deutschebahn. Our presentation was, of course, in German but, unusually, I was asked to lead part of it in English. Subsequently, the models and drawings for all six schemes were displayed in one of the giant halls in Stuttgart, which was where we made our final presentation under arc lights and with cameras!

We lost, but got a prize for coming second. I was desperately disappointed, as we had a very exciting scheme from both the engineering and the architectural aspects. Disappointments are part of a designer's life, of course, with many exciting schemes remaining unbuilt.

But, conversely, some come good. One such was the Eden Project. Eden is a long story – a millennium project that took over five years from inception to opening in March 2001. In essence, this huge project consists of the world's largest set of geodesic domes covering an enormous former china-clay pit at Bodelva in Cornwall. The problems surrounding ground engineering and substructure design in the pit were extremely complex and foundation digging, embankment stabilization and control of the natural water springs presented a major task for our civil engineers. The biomes (domes), linked in two sets of four separated by a restaurant link building, are of varying diameters joined by prismatic arches. The structures are all tubular steel with the domes as two-layer space frames in hex-tri-hex geometry. To give some idea of scale, the largest dome is 110 metres across and 50 metres high and the Tower of Pisa would fit easily inside. Apart from the sheer scale, probably the

3.20
Eden Project, Cornwall, with Nicholas Grimshaw & Partners, dome structure detail, 2001

greatest technological breakthrough is in the cladding. Glass would have been too heavy, with too many different panel shapes, and would not let through ultraviolet light, which is essential for the trees and plants inside. The team decided to explore a relatively new material, ETFE (ethyltetrafluoroethylene) foil – a Teflon-based, thin, tough plastic sheet that is 95 per cent transparent and lets through ultraviolet light.

This ETFE foil is ideal in many ways. It is light so that loads on the superstructure and foundations are less. It can be formed into very large panels of awkward shapes, the maximum size of panel here being 11 metres across. It forms a stiff, stable membrane by being inflated at low pressure into a 'pillow'. It is formed into discrete panel elements with an aluminium boundary frame and therefore is simple to fix to the main structure. And, finally, it has a life exceeding twenty-five years. By the way, with care, the right shoes and abseiling equipment, you can walk on it to carry out necessary but infrequent cleaning. The final outcome of the Eden Project, as it is called, is the most exciting and triumphant building for the whole client, design and construction team. Now see David Kirkland's Chapter 4 for architects description of the same project.

Chapter 4

A process-oriented architecture

David Kirkland, Nicholas Grimshaw & Partners Ltd

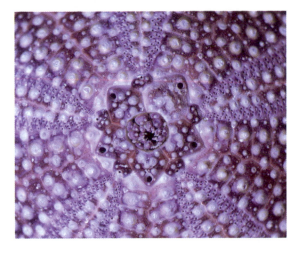

Throughout the history of architecture, built forms have tended to reflect the technologies and processes that have been within the designer's reach. Today we are on the threshold of a new era where liberation from linear processes by technology is enabling us to devise and construct complex architectural forms efficiently. Buildings no longer have to reflect the planar, orthogonal and repetitive processes of the traditional assembly line but can respond to and express the non-linear forces of nature. Such an approach will be critical if we are to design more environmentally aware buildings – the key to sustainable development. Progress within the new field of biomimetics – the abstraction of good design solutions from nature – is beginning to provide insight into how natural models can provide design solutions that are cost-effective and energy-efficient yet aesthetically elegant.

Introduction

Architecture in the developed world is in the process of undergoing dramatic and fundamental change. The drivers for this change appear to be, on the one hand, liberating new technologies and, on the other, perhaps at a deeper level, the desire to be released from the boundaries and constraints of Modernist architecture. Such constraints have been a dominant force throughout the twentieth century. Over the course of a number of years I have observed that this desire for liberation extends beyond freedom from the stylistic boundaries of the Modern Movement (and all its progeny) into a release from the physical forces of climate and gravity. In my experience as a teacher I have noticed that many students feel a desire to break the restriction of gravity. One could almost say that the planar aspect of floors tends to stifle creativity. These traits tend to remain for the duration of one's professional life, always there in the background but always restrained by the reality of capital (and physical) constraints. Perhaps the vestiges of Modernism still prevail in the search for the ephemeral. Transparency and lightness dominate.

From within this desire is emerging an architecture that seeks to express itself in non-linear form. New types of spaces are being created that have more in common with organic forms found in nature than those in the mechanistic man-made world. Architects, according to an article printed recently in the *Independent* newspaper, are looking for the 'next big thing'.

For me it seems clear that the most important issue facing the profession currently (and perhaps the most important for centuries) is sustainability. What was an issue far from most architects' minds less than fifteen years ago has now emerged as a serious agenda. Green architecture has, until recently, portrayed itself in one of two inadequate ways to the layperson: either as an unsophisticated, primitive lifestyle that has much in common with developing-world shanty towns or as an ultra high-tech 'product' that cannot be developed within normal budgetary confines. The level of debate has now intensified thanks to the widespread media coverage of the earth summits held in Rio and Kyoto.

Climate change and global warming have now become established facts and the architectural profession has the skills to make recognizable contributions to the emergence of a sustainable world. Sustainable architecture could be the catalyst required to move forward to the 'next big thing'. The difference this time is that there will be no 'stylistic' drivers. An appropriate architecture will 'evolve' from iterative steps towards more optimal solutions.

Despite what we as architects tend to think about the development of architectural movements, it is clear that tools and techniques have always played the leading role in pushing the bounds of the possible. An environmentally aware architecture will be no different. We cannot escape the fact that at the heart of what we do is the art of making.

Nature's process

As a young child I was raised in Africa and spent my formative years far away from the usual benefits of technology and civilization. Despite the standing jokes it was true that natural resources like sticks and earth were common playthings. Such immersion in the natural world brought with it a thirst for a deeper understanding of how nature works, how things are made and how, despite their absolute economy of means, they can be so beautiful. The natural world and all its splendour presented to me an infinitely complex design that had at its disposal such minimal resources yet was able to 'manufacture' solutions so finely tuned to necessity that they instilled a deep sense of awe. Watching termites or weaverbirds building their nests generated in me a desire to replicate their 'designs' with whatever resource was available to me.

Many hours were spent creating huts from twigs. The challenge was to see how far one could make a roof span with nothing more than 5-millimetre-diameter twigs and banana leaves. Invariably, like many of the great innovative buildings of history, they would collapse after a few gusts of wind. Such failure energized us to develop more

4.4
Weaverbird

Design success in the West tends to be measured in units of 'power' or 'size'. It is fair to say that a Porsche car travelling at over 200 miles per hour is, by any measure, a fantastic achievement that on a superficial level does not appear to have any natural competition. Look deeply enough at nature's full array and we find that particles travelling at the speed of light set a benchmark far and above the humanly possible. A cheetah, the fastest animal on earth, cannot match the speed of the Porsche but its acceleration of 0–60 miles per hour in almost 5 seconds comes remarkably close.

When we alter our measure of performance away from 'power' to 'efficiency' we begin to uncover how far behind we are with our own technological solutions. In closed loop systems like those we find in nature, high fluxes are abhorred – they cannot be sustained and therefore aren't. But we design open systems that are subject to high fluxes. One of these fluxes is now commonly referred to as global warming. Nature asks itself questions of appropriateness and through its feedback loops it listens and responds with answers. Such answers may well not include human beings.

Technologies that take this design process on board are demonstrating that remarkable efficiencies are possible. The cyclist Bruce Bursford achieved a speed of 334.6 kilometres per hour on a bicycle designed using ground-breaking technologies. For a lucky few, the dream of flying under one's own power is edging closer to reality and although it may not be quite bird-like, human-powered flight has nonetheless arrived.

Relying on ultra-lightweight yet incredibly strong space-age materials, modern-day pilot-powered craft such as Daedalus 88 fly with wingspans of 32 metres yet weigh only 34 kilograms. Record flights have distanced over 115 kilometres (70 miles) and lasted for almost four hours. Though meagre by the standards of commercial planes with engines that deliver more than 10,000,000 watts, these

substantial solutions. The environment is a great arbiter of success and the prototype proved to be a critical tool in the success of any endeavour. Feedback loops in nature drive the evolutionary process towards more successful solutions.

When I observed the skill local people displayed in constructing their world, it occurred to me that they showed an intuition not far removed from that of termites or weaverbirds. And they too produced fantastically appropriate solutions for their needs from scant resources. Such processes are, I believe, inherent in nature. They are an emergent phenomenon. I believe that, as an extension of nature, we too have this ability inherent within ourselves. I have come to the conclusion that there is nothing in our technological world that cannot be outdone by nature.

4.5
**Gossamer Albatross 2
human-powered aircraft**

achievements are remarkable given that the engine-pilot can sustain only enough power, fuelled by nothing more than a few bananas and a bowl of pasta, to illuminate a few light bulbs. This new generation of human-powered machines is slowly pushing technology into the realization that a 'less-is-more' philosophy generally outweighs a 'bigger-is-better' one. Such a philosophy will be frugal with its natural resources and will be careful to draw only on nature's interest, not its capital. This approach to design fits hand in glove with the requirements of a sustainable world and I am convinced that it will bring about a sea change in architectural form and thinking.

4.6
**Daedelus human-powered
aircraft**
NASA

The art of making

The way we make things, our understanding of the materials and processes involved, has always been the foundation of great architecture. As a student, I spent some time studying at the Illinois Institute of Technology in Chicago. At the time Postmodernism was the dominating architectural style and IIT was considered with general disdain by the then current establishment. The courses had not changed much in the thirty or so years since Mies van der Rohe had been active there. An early memorable experience of my first week was of my tutor, Alfred Caldwell – a wonderful and wise teacher who had worked with both Mies and Frank Lloyd Wright – breaking, with a trembling hand, his pencil in two as he tried to draw a large, violent cross over my house elevation, executed in the style of Michael Graves – all pink and purple. For an eighty-five year old in the peaceful twilight years of his life I thought that this was perhaps a little excessive. Needless to say the merits and longevity of the architectural course were less to do with style and form and more to do with making and detail. It was primarily an education about the process of making.

The education was developed around seeking an understanding of structure and detail and how solving these issues appropriately led to well-proportioned and elegant architectural form. When developing designs for a brick house, many hours were spent solving complex junctions with bags of small timber bricks called 'Mies's pieces'. Longer-span architectural problems likewise were solved with the aid of accurate brass sections soldered together. Prototypes and mock-ups were an intrinsic aspect of the course and through this iterative process one could see how optimal solutions emerged. In Chicago, being surrounded by such fine examples of Mies' work, the process became evident in the architecture.

Clearly the architectural intent was informed by the technology available at the time. Crown Hall, for me, expresses the nature of standardized, planar components. The largest sheets of rectangular glass and standard steel sections come together to form one of the most beautiful examples of 'planar' architecture. The beauty of this building transcends its logic in a way that very few examples of that age have been able to achieve. So many buildings rigorously applied these principles but failed to achieve the sublime.

The role of the engineer

The work of Fazler Kahn, the great engineer responsible for making much of Mies' and Myron Goldsmith's architecture work so elegantly, had a great influence on me at an early stage in my education. The master stroke of using the secondary roof purlins to brace the primary beams on Crown Hall enabled the classical elegance and proportion of this building to work so finely. The role of the engineer has always been undervalued in the design process and for me all good buildings are an example of a very close and equal dialogue between the two skills. Any educational system that does not seek actively to promote this is, I think, destined to move the architectural profession further away from reality. Environmental engineers are now rightly being regarded with equality as we begin to understand the symbiotic nature of 'efficiency' in sustainable design.

On returning from Chicago, I strove to continue this 'art of making' process at the Royal College of Art in London and whilst there was fortunate to have Michael Dickson of Buro Happold as a tutor, assisting with structural design. My studies tended towards developing structural solutions that were lightweight, efficient and standardized. The aim of these studies did not, however, end there. I attempted to find a way of liberating these designs from orthogonal planes and forms into more free-form and organic shapes. There had to be a way of doing this with standardized components and, through a project brief to design a 1980s version of the Crystal Palace in Hyde Park, positive developments began to take place. It was this project that led to a long passion for large-span enclosures.

This was the first time that I became aware of ETFE (Ethyltetrafluoroethylene) foil, which was eventually to be used on the Eden Project. Michael Dickson had done some work using this material and it took him a long while before he managed to convince me that such a material actually existed. It seemed to me that ETFE fell into the same category as many 'wonder' materials students tend to use – something that existed in small samples on researcher's workbenches but would not be available for years. Finally we had a material that was transparent, light-weight, insulative and yet could be patterned into complex forms. Bucky Fuller's vision was now available.

The developments of the Crystal Palace design evolved into a scheme basically configured as a tensile 'spine' truss that separated out straight compressive struts with tensile cables. By altering the lengths of each cable varying geometries could be generated. A standard cast node was developed that could be used for all connections. The internal accommodation system would also use the same components.

Looking back on these designs, one can begin to see that their naivety stemmed from a lack of fabrication and construction experience. With hindsight, however, it is possible to see them as small but progressive steps that had to be taken in order to move along a refining path. From the RCA I began working with Nicholas Grimshaw & Partners, who had just been commissioned to design the Eurostar International Terminal at Waterloo. I was fortunate in that Nick was aware of my interest in long-span structures and sought to develop this by giving me responsibility for designing the station roof.

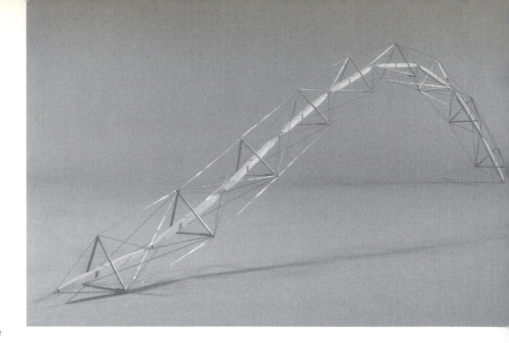

The Grimshaw design process

Perhaps the most interesting thing about this firm's design process is the involvement of engineers, fabricators and constructors at the earliest stages of new projects. There exists within the office a remarkable passion and understanding of the art of 'making' architecture. It is this that is the driver for all the most successful projects the office has completed. There is less concern for formal or stylistic solutions to problems and a greater reliance on the process of design and development and the faith that following this course of action and managing problems creatively results in 'optimal' solutions. A process-oriented architecture is one that seeks to allow these 'forces' to influence not hinder the design process. These forces are many and vary from project to project but will always include issues and limitations of manufacture, cost, transportation, erection, orientation and environment. The solutions respond positively to these forces and do not seek to fight them.

In the last few years the practice has been developing a design process that is more environmentally driven, with an emphasis on creating buildings that are sustainable yet at the same time beautiful and sophisticated.

4.7
Non-uniform tensile spine truss made from standard components: student project for a new Crystal Palace, Royal College of Art, 1985

Indigenous architecture

Some of the best and simplest examples of this process-oriented approach can be seen in indigenous vernacular buildings. Most are as striking as any natural form and are not only remarkable structures demonstrating a complete understanding of the (usually) limited materials used but are also ingenious low-energy passive environmental solutions – and rich in cultural significance. This architecture can be thought of as a real extension of nature and its lineage can be traced from primitive times to now, albeit very faintly for most of history.

The evolution of the glasshouse

In seeking to communicate how this environmentally responsive, process-driven design method can be demonstrated in physical form I have found that the development of glasshouse design proves to be a very succinct example of how building forms respond to the natural world. They have very simple criteria – to maximize solar light and heat gain and minimize heat loss. The question is how far can the building form assist towards maximizing free energy. A unit of measure should be established to compare this in the same way that human-powered flight can be compared with carbon-powered machines.

Waterloo International Terminal is perhaps, for me, one of the most intriguing examples of process-oriented architecture because, as an extension of the evolution of large glass buildings, the terminal's roof structure has a form that has been little seen since the early nineteenth century. The glazing of complex three-dimensional surfaces relies heavily on an understanding of the limitations of manufacture and construction techniques. Some of the early glasshouses such as Bicton (1820) are highly crafted buildings that pushed, and indeed expressed, the limitations of the glass-manufacturing processes of the time. The 'crown' process of glass manufacture produced only limited sizes of glass pane (up to 0.75

metres x 0.5 metres but generally much smaller) and it was only after manufacturers began employing the new 'cylinder' process in the 1830s that glass sheet size increased to around 1.0 metres x l.3 metres. The fact that each sheet of glass could be cut *in situ* allowed complex forms to be erected.

The morphology of these early glasshouses was largely established by physical and environmental requirements. For me, these buildings are the 'gene bank' for modern, environmentally responsive building forms. Indeed, most glasshouses were conceived without the input of architects, who tended to produce their designs in Grecian or Gothic styles – beautiful monuments devoid of any dialogue with the natural environment and its harvestable resources. In an effort to produce minimal structures, greatly reducing interference with light, composite-shell construction was pushed to the limit and used to great effect, albeit with catastrophic consequences at times. All these structures were only possible because of J. C. Loudon's revolutionary iron sash bar design – the ground-breaking technology of the time. Harsh, corrosive, internal environments, however, eventually saw a return to the use of timber.

As the glass-manufacturing process changed and standardization became the norm, so the morphology shifted back to being planar, Joseph Paxton's Crystal Palace perhaps being the pinnacle of this type. The staggering nine-month programme was only achieved because of this shift in technology from craft to mass production. Interestingly this building was also influenced by nature. Paxtons' intricate structure was modelled on the form of water lily leaves. Very little has changed in glasshouse form as the processes are still highly standardized. Perhaps the biggest change has been the development of toughened glass, allowing greater clear spans. The flip side to this benefit has been the decline of cutting *in situ*, perhaps severing all craft-based approaches.

Most glasshouses designed today still display planar forms and when one assesses these buildings from an environmental point of view we can clearly see that such a strategy is less than optimal. Before the days of energy conservation this was perhaps not a big issue but heat loss and solar gain for this building type are big issues. Planar buildings do not respond very effectively to the natural environment. Sunlight is only able to penetrate fully at one time of the day. All other times will see increasing degrees of reflection. Solar penetration is compromised.

The international rail terminal at Waterloo

Like the original Crystal Palace design, the roof at Waterloo International Terminal was also to be constructed in nine months. From very early on in the design stages it became obvious that the site profile, dictated by the track alignment, would influence all our subsequent decisions. Because of this complexity and the unknown knock-on effects further down the design and construction process, it became clear that the wisest course of action would be to flow with the problems as opposed to forcing them into a predetermined solution. Geometry, flexibility and buildability were to become the key to success and it was a thorough understanding of fabrication, manufacturing and building processes that enabled lateral solutions to be found. Like Paxton's Crystal Palace, standardization was to be critical for success and the key problem was to reconcile this with a very irregular morphology.

A solution was reached that enabled 230 out of a total of 1,680 glass panels to be 'standard' rectangles. Each panel overlapped each vertically adjacent panel much like snake scales. The key to eliminating geometric twist was the incorporation of a standard neoprene concertina gasket, which could accommodate out-of-plane variances of approximately 80 millimetres. Each panel was fixed

to the external steelwork via a series of standard interconnecting stainless-steel castings. These connections were assembled from four independently rotating components, allowing a variance in position of 180 millimetres in each axis.

Critical to the workability of this solution was the use of models and mock-ups to generate artificially a physical evolution of the design. During the intermediate design stages a full-scale prototype of a roof bay, complete with cladding, was erected at the steel fabricator's works. This required many attempts before the final details emerged. Like the natural world, the feedback from each iteration contributed to an evolutionary process.

The design that resulted was of a highly irregular geometry, constructed of standard components and built in nine months. For me, it was perhaps the most significant major glass building for nearly 120 years because it established a continuation of the genetic line that first emerged in the organic forms of early London glasshouses.

The Eden Project

After Waterloo was completed it struck me that in any architectural office there would be very few comparable projects. At precisely this time a chap called Tim Smit walked into our office and presented us with his dream of creating the largest glasshouse the world has ever seen. What initially looked like a pipe dream began to look more and more like a viable project. Tim had the passion, commitment and energy to make things happen. He had an uncanny ability to rally people to the cause and if anybody could make it happen it was he. However, passion can only take a design so far and in the office the excitement of designing such a dream began to shift towards concern as we came to realize that the brief could not be sustained by the capital cost. This was to be one of many issues that severely tested the design team, and fairly early on it became apparent

4.8
Waterloo International Terminal, London, 1993 (architect: Nicholas Grimshaw & Partners)

4.9
Glass panels

4.10
Eden Project, Cornwall, 2001: interior fog (architect: Nicholas Grimshaw & Partners)

that if a solution were to be found it would need to evolve out of lateral responses to the problems at hand. Fortunately, the same design team that had worked on Waterloo were now on board and the lessons learnt from our process-driven experience proved to be the nursery for Eden.

For us, perhaps the single most difficult issue was the site itself. Tim had found an isolated clay pit that was coming to the end of its life and this immediately presented a wonderful opportunity to raise an ecological project from reclaimed industrial wasteland. Nothing could be seen of the site itself until one stood at the very edge of the pit. Once there, the view was breathtaking. Here was a landscape that resembled the 'lost world' of Conan Doyle. The drama of the site itself was enough to

attract visitors. Such drama, of course, had its down side: designing and constructing such a huge building and ensuring that it contributed to and did not destroy this asset was to prove extremely difficult.

Many early schemes fell by the wayside as it emerged that they could not provide satisfactory solutions for the issues of cost and buildability. Those that could proved to be severely compromised from an architectural point of view. Quite clearly the brief had called for the building to be an example of world-class architecture, ranking alongside those glasshouse greats of the nineteenth century. Because of the nature of the funding mechanisms for the project, a detailed design and cost plan had to be in place, proving viability, before any significant capital could be released to develop the project. We were caught between a rock and a hard place because without the financial assets significant design development could not take place.

This issue was further compounded by the fact that the site itself could not be purchased and controlled until financial closure with the funders. Up until that point it was still being mined at an alarming rate. Usually the one thing an architect can be

confident of is that the ground is fixed and will only move upon instruction. Our stamina began to be severely tested as time and again we would visit the site with well-developed layouts only to find our proposals to be floating in mid-air, on one or two occasions by as much as 20 metres.

A design strategy had to be found that could simultaneously provide all the certainties yet have sufficient flexibility to allow for alterations and detail development at a later stage. A 'genetic code' had to be found. Again, faced with 'forces' a league on from those we experienced at Waterloo we concentrated on developing a solution to satisfy each. With luck, careful and creative management of these solutions would also provide us with a satisfactory architecture. It was very clear, however, that there could be no inefficiencies whatsoever: any design solution would be pared right to the bone and our architecture would need to be an emergent rather than a willful one. In many ways this architecture was to be less about 'form follows function' and more to do with 'form follows environment' – a good guiding principle for a sustainable approach to building forms.

Nature as model and mentor

We spent many days poring over past studies of minimal structures and began turning again to the book of nature for answers. Perhaps the two most important observations of natural systems to influence us were: how nature's designs are so elegant yet so sparing; and that in nature most solutions fulfill more than function.

From the outset of the project we had wanted to ensure that the architecture would contribute to the Eden Project story; it should be more than a container into which exhibits would be poured. Since the core message of the project is one of sustainability, it was important to develop a design that could, regardless of size, be considered sustainable. Studies of bubble and foam structures demonstrated to us the

4.11
Eden Project: castings

efficiency of spherical geometries. Minimum surface area for maximum volume sounded like an economic strategy that was going to be hard to beat. This benefit was compounded by the inherent efficiency of geodesic structural geometries.

These efficiencies extended beyond the structure and into the envelope and environmental systems. Spheres are minimal surfaces that have maximum volume. They also, unlike more common orthogonal glasshouse forms, allow direct sunlight to enter perpendicular to the surface at all times of the day, thus maximizing the free energy.

The ability of current desktop computers to carry out complex calculations enabled us to undertake solar animation studies for the pit. We studied 365 days to provide an accurate and essential solar profile. Maximizing solar penetration was a key target and knowing where this asset lay determined the optimal positions for the biome structures. The results of this mapping indicated that our design should be linear in profile with lean-to structures built against south-facing cliffs. Such a diagram refers back to the very earliest glasshouse structures, such as Bicton. (One can only wonder at what ephemeral designs would have been developed by these engineers had they had access to the sophisticated form-finding software we have now.) Not wanting to abandon the supreme efficiency of spherical structures, we replicated foam geometries by linking bubbles in three dimensions, carefully following our solar boundaries whilst ensuring that the brief areas could be sustained.

Having accepted that the ground profiles would be constantly changing we developed a three-dimensional computer model that could be continually modified. The geodesic spheres were 'pushed' into a ground profile model and the resulting intersection line extrapolated and approximated to the nearest hexagonal panel. As the ground profiles altered over the months this intersection line adjusted accordingly and panels

were added or subtracted as required. Throughout this process the remaining 90 per cent of the building remained fixed and this could then be developed and resolved to a greater level of detail and cost certainty. Perhaps most important for us was the fact that the architecture could be established and was safe. No cost or programme penalties would emerge as the site continued to be mined.

From an architectural point of view one of our biggest concerns was the resolution of intersecting spherical geometries. The truss lines could not be made to have matching geometries on either side, and to an architect, particularly one educated within the Meisian system, this proves to be a very uncomfortable issue. Not wanting to compromise the efficiency of our structure, we again studied nature for possible solutions and eventually came across a dragonfly's wing as a model for how minimal surfaces (which when packed tend to form hexagons) intersect with straight edges such as support ribs. The geometries on either side of the ribs are not symmetrical yet the performance is not compromised and the wing remains aesthetically elegant. Such a model proved to be a lesson for us, demonstrating that we sometimes have a single-minded view of geometry and elegance.

Further efficiencies were gained when we began to assess the options available for transparent cladding systems. Upon analysis, double-glazing on this scale and in this form proved to be less than satisfactory and the design was developed using ETFE foil – a transparent Teflon foil system fabricated as triple-skin pillows inflated to 300 pounds per square inch. These pillows allow greater penetration of low-frequency ultraviolet light, are better thermal conductors and weigh less than 1 per cent of double-glazed glass panels. Maximum panel size on the biomes is 53 square metres, which greatly reduced the weight of primary steel structure and its subsequent shading effect. The downside of this system is lifespan, which is estimated at twenty-five years –

4.12

4.13

4.13

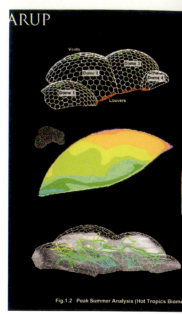

Fig.1.2 Peak Summer Analysis (Hot Tropics Biome

4.15

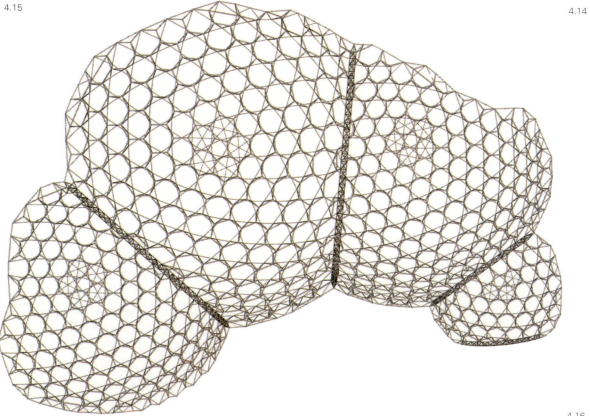

4.14

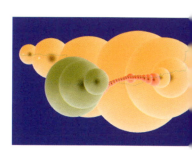

4.16

fairly low relative to glass. However, it is commonly known that the weakest link in any double-glazed panels is the silicone seal, estimated at about twenty to twenty-five years, which should only be replaced under factory conditions. A quick calculation actually shows that the volume of foil used to enclose the biomes is almost that of the silicon joints that would be required for double-glazing, when flattened to an equivalent 0.3 millimetres. The foil panel, however, is designed to be replaced easily by two people and without expensive cranes.

Biomimetics

In having sought efficient and elegant solutions from nature for both the Eden Project and Waterloo I am now more intrigued than ever at the amazing potential that lies untapped. Such a resource is surely more valuable than gold and the techniques for 'mining' it are emerging within the new field of biomimetics. The fullness of genuine 'natural architecture' for me has less to do with having a floor plan laid out in the pattern of a nautilus shell or with using natural untreated materials and more to do with working within the same parameters or 'design' processes as nature.

If chaos theory transformed our view of the universe, biomimicry is set to transform the way we live on Earth. It is the quest for innovation inspired by nature. The field is forged by scientists and innovators who study nature's wonders – spider silk and seashells, photosynthesis and forests – and adapt them for human use. And their findings are revolutionizing the way we compute, harness energy and transport and heal ourselves.

Spider silk, for example, is considered one of nature's wonder materials. Biomimeticists seek to discover how it performs so well when compared to our manmade 'wonder' materials like Kevlar. Ounce for ounce it is five times stronger than steel. Kevlar is made from petroleum at great pressure and

temperatures of several hundred degrees. Concentrated sulphuric acid is used in the process and the by-products are highly toxic. By comparison, however, spiders make silk at room temperature and pressure, without corrosive or toxic by-products and, most remarkably of all, they make it from chewed up grasshoppers and flies. Finding the key to such processes will reap benefits for both business and the environment. Architecture must surely be one of the greatest benefactors in such a revolution.

In *Biomimicry: Innovation inspired by nature* (New York: William Morrow, 1997), science writer Janine Benyus states three key factors that describe this new field of study:

> Biomimicry studies nature's models and then imitates or takes inspiration from these designs and processes to solve human problems. It uses an ecological standard to judge the 'rightness' of our innovations. After 3.8 billion years of evolution, nature has learned: What works? What is appropriate? What lasts? And finally it is a new way of viewing and valuing nature. It introduces an era based not on what we can extract from the natural world, but on what we can learn from it.

Summary

For me these principles extend beyond what we would term the 'natural' world and into the 'man-made'. The principles that govern how a termite or weaverbird builds its nest, using the resources it has available in the most efficient manner, with little or no waste, whilst harnessing what free energy is available, extends into indigenous vernacular architecture. The supreme elegance and efficiency of an Inuit igloo is a benchmark of appropriateness. Computational Fluid Dynamics studies carried out by Arup have shown that, when it comes to issues of internal temperature, carbon monoxide and humidity,

4.12
Eden Project, Cornwall, 2001: cross-section showing how the building changes with the rising and lowering of the ground profiles

4.13
Analysis of the thermal dynamics of the Humid Tropics Biome during the summer months

4.14
Early concept diagram demonstrating how a sphere intersects the ground plane

4.14
Plan of Humid Tropics Biomes

4.16
The ETFE foil cladding

this form, made from nothing more than snow, is truly amazing. One wonders at what architects like us today would produce given the same brief and resource. The great Gothic cathedrals demonstrate, granted for a different brief, the immense potential of another simple and abundant resource – stone.

It would be exciting to think that a building like the Eden Project, with a total weight less than that of the air inside, could be considered within a similar category of process-oriented architecture, but when measured against the work of termites, Inuits, Amerindians, spiders and bicycles it is only a beginning. What is really exciting, however, is to know the potential that exists – the potential to create truly sustainable architecture that emerges from a deep understanding of nature, to create forms no longer restrained by classical and Cartesian thought but system based, responsive and evolving. If we tap into nature's processes and methodology and combine them with the materials, resources and computing power available to us now it is easy to imagine how we could be on the threshold of a new architecture – one that is humane, pollution- and emission-free, resourceful and economic, efficient and elegant, and truly effective. The forms of such an architecture, I am convinced, will be more akin to those found in nature than those of the industrial age.

Conclusion

It seems to me that at the core of our current environmental crisis is the loss of relationship with the natural order. Ask most people living in the developed world when was the last time that they experienced a sense of awe at nature's wonder and they tend to struggle for a minute or two. Yet, no matter where we look, on close inspection we see the same dynamic process unfolding. The whole of nature seems to be speaking a language beyond the confines of any human tongue and the biomimeticist's role is that of translating it for us.

When we learn to play by nature's rules we will again become aligned to its process and order and our precarious position will once again come into balance. Such a message is not new, yet it is only recently that we have been able to grasp that such change, hard as it may seem, has the potential actually to bring about tremendous economic growth. Efficiency, we are learning, is essential in any economic enterprise. Designing a building to use 50 per cent less energy over a twenty-five-year lifespan can only bring economic benefit to its owner. When these life-cycle costs are compared to initial capital costs we begin to see how such design strategies can really alter the quality of our economic and built environments.

Architects, it seems to me, have a key role in forging ahead and bringing about the required beneficial change to the present order and, far from being handicapped by such strategies, our creative abilities will be opened up to new territories. Such territories have been on the horizon for the last thirty years. We now have the tools, technologies and economic strategies finally to make the next 'evolutionary' step in architecture for the real benefit of people and the environment in which we live.

Janine Benyus observes that the biomimeticist's notebook can be summarized by the following commandments:

– Nature runs on sunlight
– Nature uses only the energy it needs
– Nature fits form to function
– Nature recycles everything
– Nature rewards competition
– Nature banks on diversity
– Nature demands local expertise
– Nature curbs excesses from within
– Nature taps the power of limits.

The day is surely upon us when, cultural issues aside, we can imagine the words 'man's endeavour' beginning to replace the word 'nature'.

Chapter 5

Material innovation and the development of form

Mark Lovell, Mark Lovell Design Engineers

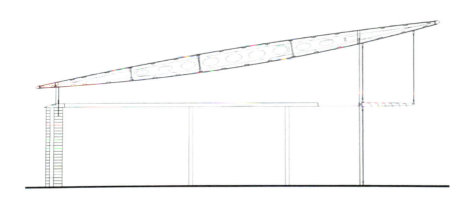

5.1
Radiant House, Energy World Exhibition, Milton Keynes, 1994: cross-section (architect: Richard Weston)

Mankind, from the beginning of time, has developed uses and applications for all materials as they have become available. Intrinsically the creativity of the human brain has always striven to extract the maximum benefit from any resource. The extreme pressure to survive would have been a powerful incentive to minimize the amount of material and level of effort to achieve the function required. Initial lessons would have been learned from observing nature and its forms and structures. A simple replication of nature's forms with substances of a similar type would have yielded good levels of success.

This type of process is currently being relearned

and has been applied to many newly acclaimed and award-winning buildings. The synergy has been acknowledged with the title 'organic design'. In the case of primitive man the title 'natural design' might be more applicable, as the process avoided direct waste. Such an approach became highly developed in early tribes, especially those that needed to move to sustain their lifestyle. Shelter being one of the primary needs, each tribe would develop an appropriate response based on their local materials.

The 'yurt' used by the Mongols was a lightweight, easily transportable dwelling that could quickly be disassembled, transported by horse and re-erected. It was circular in form, with a conical roof and generally around 3 or 4 metres in diameter. The outer wall was constructed from panels of articulated hinged slats that opened out to create a strong and light herringbone structure. This perimeter hoop formed a rim on which a lightweight timber and skin roof could be supported. It was not uncommon for the roof to have twin skins of material to assist with environmental control within the dwelling. The form of the yurt helped spawn the Dymaxion House created by Buckminster Fuller in about 1929.

Many other tribes around the globe developed their own type of dwelling. Some of these, such as Bedouin tents, used tensile forms. This type of

5.4 left
Puffin Aircraft during man-powered flight

5.5 right
Radiant House, Energy World Exhibition, Milton Keynes, 1994: interior view

5.2 left, upper
Wing section under construction in the workshop

5.3 left, lower
Transportation of prefabricated wing section

dwelling combined tensile and compressive materials to achieve the required structural parameters.

Viking ships used clinker-formed hulls whereby strips of wood were joined together to form a thin, weathertight and efficient structural skin. The shell is an efficient form and the creativity of man was needed to create large sheets of timber so that the form could be realized. This philosophy was repeated many centuries later when steel was first produced in small sheets: a riveted form of construction was conceived to create large elements for structures such as the Forth Bridge. The Airstream caravan is similar in constructional form, using aluminium sections.

The primitive coracle was a small boat that used a single animal skin stretched over a lightweight timber frame. Its jointless construction was watertight and created a highly transportable boat for a single person to ford rivers and lakes. The extremely robust and efficient Mosquito aircraft is a flying modern-day version of this material form of construction. Most things have been done before! As an engineer, I find that these early designs inspire new variations in both formal and material terms.

Radiant House, built for the Energy World Exhibition in Milton Keynes and designed by architect

Richard Weston in 1994, refers to Alvar Aalto, adopting many of his principles in an extremely clean modern form. As the project engineer for this building, I felt it was important to develop a strong, readable structural philosophy to strengthen the architectural language. We developed a roof based on the idea of an aeroplane wing that floats overhead providing protection like a beneficent cloud. The roof is supported solely by slender glass walls. The front glass wall represents one of the first complex engineering uses of glass whereby it clearly performs the function of a slender compressive column in combination with a bending beam element.

The structural simplicity of this transparent solution strongly supports the architectural statement. The structural scheme and architectural language are harmoniously working together to create a memorable building. The careful selection of the construction materials has given something subliminal to the project.

The glass columns are extremely slender, with a ratio of around 400: parameters greater than 250 are unusual. The fundamental nature of glass and its natural compressive strength appealed to my engineering instincts. The use of this material in this location clearly displays its function in holding the roof above the ground. This function is offset by the five-millimetre-diameter tension wires around the building perimeter that hold the roof down. It would have been possible to use the limited tensile capacity of the glass to perform this function but the glass panels would have needed to be drilled with fixing holes, significantly increasing the cost and overall assembly complexity. It was decided to separate and express clearly each function and add to the readable language of the building. The integration of truly structural glass members with other materials was also a novel feature. The glass panels were all made to different widths to reflect Aalto's interest in 'the randomness of the forest'.[1]

Radiant House has a powerful visual and functional form. This is underpinned by a strong but unseen traditional craft approach. The roof form uses similar principles to those used for the Mosquito aircraft. It is made from a series of glued and screwed timber elements pieced together with a plywood outer skin (the Mosquito had a fabric skin). To achieve the final form, full and half-size templates were made as 'shadow graphs' to review the shape and profile. Shadow graphs are created in the aircraft industry to check for form irregularities. These are usually checked at fifty times life size. The eye is an incredible checking instrument and can discern the smallest deviation from the correct form. Drawing elements at an exaggerated scale, either small or large depending on the item, can be beneficial and assist the evaluation process

During its early stages the president of Kymmene Finland became aware of the design of this Finnish pavilion and encouraged its realization by offering free A-grade all-lamination plywood. This gesture helped to limit the financial difference between the traditional approach and a more cost-effective steel-frame solution.

Radiant House required some special ingredients to be completed using traditional skills. Generally, all noteworthy projects need three main ingredients: a good client, a good design team and a good builder. If any of these ingredients are missing the full potential of the project cannot be realized. A construction skill not commonly available in the building industry was wing fabrication. To assist the construction process a retired aeronautical engineer, James Say, was introduced to the builder to help the craftsmen adapt their skills to the needs of this aeronautically inspired structure. His experience of building Second World War timber fighter aircraft and the highly acclaimed Puffin Aircraft was brought to bear.

The Puffin was an incredible milestone for lightweight man-powered aeronautical timber engineering. The aircraft had an 83-foot wingspan and a net weight of only 118 pounds! Design work started in the mid-1950s and at the beginning of the 1960s it was nearly the first man-powered aircraft to fly a complete figure of eight and win the Kramer Prize of £5,000. Some 1,100 3/4 yards around the test track one of its wings touched a parked car and it crashed. The challenge was finally achieved by others some twenty-five years later.

James Say's experience gave the builder the information he needed to build the construction jigs, which allowed the 2.4-metre modules that made up the roof to be reproduced accurately. Mr Say specified that lighter and thinner material should be used if we were ever to construct another roof using similar principles. The actual choice of material was limited to the thicknesses of wood kindly donated by Kymmene's president.

The three components required for a good project described earlier are usually hard to find in combination. There was a further complication on this project: time. The building had to be conceived, designed and constructed in only eleven weeks, all with the help of 150 kilograms of glue. The project was designed and built within the deadline, although the kitchen and bathrooms were not fitted. The lead-in period for the project was three days! The

5.6
**Oyster House, Ideal Home
Exhibition, London,
1997–8**

timescale was unrealistically short under normal circumstances but the team was very committed and the goals were achieved. The office resource capacity did not exist and most items were designed overnight and faxed through to the contractor each morning. A larger project or one taking place over a longer period could not have been sustained in this manner.

This project also revealed builder's phobias towards glass. The walls are made from 15-millimetre-thick toughened glass, which is very strong and very durable apart from in a few special cases. The workmen were on occasions too reverential and had to be persuaded that the glass was not too delicate to perform its designated tasks.

The selection of materials for projects needs careful consideration. Many innovative schemes appear to the outsider to be revolutionary but this is far from reality. On a like-for-like basis compared with similar projects carried out by others they are revolutionary. But on a person level, each project is a progressive, systematical development from the last. Good engineering in most cases in the construction industry is evolutionary rather than revolutionary.

The timber monocoque form has been well developed within the modern design idiom. Working with Cowley Structural Timber Ltd, Mark Lovell Design Engineers (MLDE) designed and built the reading pods on the acclaimed Peckham Library project to a performance specification. The pods consisted of Kerto ribs structurally skinned with OSB (oriented strand board) plywood on the inside and outside faces. The shell uses the plywood as stressed skin elements. The three-dimensional natural form efficiently creates a very strong and stiff structure. Experience from Radiant House and other similar schemes assisted the development of this form. The free-form shell was extremely demanding in terms of the amount of time needed to produce fabrication drawings and the manufacturing resources required. The assembly process was repetitive but each component had a unique form.

With the same manufacturer MLDE created the structure for the Oyster House at the *Daily Mail* Ideal Home Exhibition. This building was extremely innovative in material terms and constructional terms. The floors and roof are designed in composite, plywood-faced, Styrofoam-cored structural panels. In the perimeter areas there are curved structural composite panel units. The engineering is dependent on the quality of the glue technology. The thin lightweight structures provided excellent thermal performance. The column connectors designed for this project were patented by the fabricator and are now used on a variety of lamella and grid-shell-type structures.

Two-dimensional curved structures are much simpler to manufacture and produce than three-dimensional ones and generally still contain the elegance and grace of the more complex forms, especially when constructed in timber. Good timber structures have a subliminal strength that adds to their visual quality.

The A4 Millennium Bridge between Calne and Chippenham, designed and engineered by MLDE, portrays the visual qualities of the simple arch. The structure uses a glue-laminated redwood section for the main arch member and a deck structure manufactured from Kerto Q. The associated metalwork has a simple galvanized finish to give a low-cost, durable protective coating. This structure would be impossible to build without the materials

5.7
Reading pods, designed by MLDE for Peckham Library, London, 2000 (architect: Alsop and Störmer)

technology needed to glue all the small pieces together. The size and scale of this project required large, structural, site-glued joints to assemble the three main pieces that form the deck member, which is some 0.163 metres thick, 2.1 metres wide and nearly 40 metres long.

As a brief digression, it is well known that very little in the world is new; things are just applied differently. This famous statement is correct in most cases and provides guidance for receptive engineers. In the Victorian era, Thonet used his creative skill to solve the production problems caused by tightly bending steamed beech rods. In many cases the wood would split because of the large tension forces created. Thonet's patented process allowed mass-produced chairs, such as model No. 14, to be produced in their millions for only a few pennies each.

In broad terms three main criteria can create the backbone of a design and the process can be driven

5.8
A4 Millennium Bridge, UK, 2000

from these three main positions. The most common starting point currently chosen is form, usually driven in the first instance by the architect. The materials are then sought to realize the shape. The life expectancy and usage pattern add to these criteria. In addition, the price also influences the material choice. The lack of long-term durability of many 'high tech' schemes will become evident in the near future. Only the few projects that were carefully specification controlled will function without considerable ongoing maintenance.

The second criterion that can drive the design process is the material selection. When a new material becomes known or is invented uses are usually quickly created. The material is then exploited in the new market sectors. A new composite material invented in the latter part of the Industrial Revolution was reinforced concrete. The introduction of steel rods into concrete created a new super-material – what might have been described as 'a ductile stone with bending and tension strength': wide-scale commercial use of concrete frames did not really take place until the early 1900s.

The intrinsic characteristics of concrete as a material even up to the present day are rarely fully exploited. In strength terms it can be enormously strong. However, probably 99 per cent of the concrete used in the construction industry is specified with quite a low strength of less than 40 Newtons per square millimetre. Concrete can be quite easily produced at much higher strengths with only a small price penalty. Certain types of low-cost concrete can easily achieve compressive strengths in excess of 70 Newtons per square millimetre.

Even in one-off cases, concrete with only twice the raw material cost can be produced with a compressive strengths of 159 Newtons per square millimetre, a fivefold strength increase over normal grades. Concrete of this strength was specified by myself for an industrial client in 1996. This level of strength was reached in twenty-eight days. It is

believed that this is the strongest commercial concrete used in the UK. I am currently investigating even higher strength concrete for specific installations.

The main characteristic of concrete is its fluidity. This is rarely used but can be utilized by a variety of construction processes: forming, casting, extruding or even spraying. An example of very large pre-cast curved concrete elements can be viewed at Greenock Waterfront Leisure Complex. These elements weigh some 27 tons each and were cast in one piece. They were formed with external and internal moulds in order to achieve their highly curved and tapered shapes. They have been affectionately called 'elephant tusks' and described as 'urban sculpture'.

Concrete can also be sprayed. This is an extremely fast, cost-effective and simple method and avoids the need for expensive and elaborate formwork. However, this type of concrete application is probably the least used in the construction of buildings.

An interesting form was created by this type of construction method at Pokesdown School in Bournemouth. The architects for the school were Format Milton Architects. Five 125-millimetre-thick concrete structural light scoops two storeys high were engineered into the building fabric by myself. These elements not only structurally support the first floor and wall loads but also provide an environmental moderator that assists air distribution and improves the light levels at the back of the deep-plan classrooms. Many projects could benefit from the improved building physics criteria created by the structure.

Composite materials will be more common in the future. There will be a wide range of concrete-type materials that primarily will be recycled materials bound together. These trends are starting to develop; recycled materials such as glass and chipped car tyres are being used.

The rotary engine had been designed and conceived for many years before a real production

5.9
Greenock Waterfront Leisure Complex, 1996: concrete 'tusks' being erected (architect: FaulknerBrown)

5.10
'Tusk', reinforced-concrete cage fabrication

5.11
**Pokesdown School,
Bournemouth, 1997:
cross-section (architect:
Format Milton Architects)**

5.12
**Skyward view inside
light scoop**

5.13
**View of back of light
scoops**

model could be realized. The commercial production of extremely hard-wearing ceramic materials allowed sensible life expectancies to be achieved for the rota lobe tips. These ceramic materials are starting to be designed into buildings and are changing their forms.

The third basic approach to designing, driven neither by form nor material, is pure creativity and intensive effort. This process creates logic-driven forms and could be described as forensic innovation. A good example is Buckminster Fuller's 'Bucky Balls' or 'Fullerenes'. He developed super-efficient tensegrity structures that postulate the possibility of unknown elements. An exciting new element, Carbon 60, was later discovered by an organic chemist, and the molecule was named after Buckminster Fuller.

The changing base criterion of modern society has in most cases swept away the benchmarks set by prehistoric humans and has developed a free radical approach, the trend being that any design is good so long as it has the 'correct' appearance! In most cases the igloo approach does not now apply. In Greenland the igloo could be said to be an almost perfect solution to the human requirement for shelter. The form uses one of the most efficient compressive structural systems – the dome. The material used is sustainable and is taken directly from

the surrounding landscape and has a good compressive strength. It is quick to build, needing only simple tools to extract it from the land. The building process is also fairly straightforward and the construction material is totally recyclable.

Teletubbies-style houses are not commonplace in the landscape. Under the current acceptability criteria they are not considered suitable. The form is structurally efficient and has the minimum surface area for maximum volume and therefore has good thermal qualities. While the world's constructional material resources are not too stretched or too expensive, purely practical reasons for engineering design will carry little weight.

I stated earlier that there are three main driving criteria behind the constructed object: a desire for specific form, the creativity of the designer and the limiting characteristics of the materials. Building materials have three main structural properties: tensile, compressive and bending strengths. Most

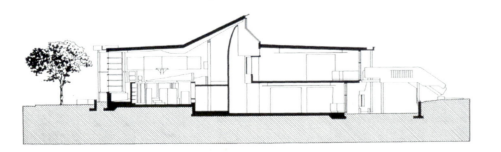

materials have a selection of these different attributes in differing amounts. Materials that exhibit tensile characteristics are carbon and natural fibres such as hemp and jute. Materials with predominantly compressive strength are glass and ceramics. Materials with good bending characteristics are steel and reinforced concrete.

The intrinsic strength of 'high-strength' materials can be significantly higher than presently utilized. Normal grade steel has a tensile strength of around 275 Newtons per square millimetre. The best commercial grade of drawn steel has a strength of around 2,300 Newtons per square millimetre. If steel can be produced without naturally occurring Griffith cracks then its strength properties are a thousand times higher! It is hard to perceive 1 square millimetre of this special steel being equivalent to 1,000 square millimetres of the normal material.

In the mid-1920s Marcel Breuer designed a series of chairs that exploited high-tensile steel tubing, which was just becoming commercially available. These chairs required the high-tensile strength offered by the chrome section frame in order to withstand the applied forces. Normal steel would buckle and yield under such stresses. The commercially available man-made fibre materials with the highest tensile strengths can withstand about 7,000 Newtons per square millimetre, a strength value about three times higher than the best steel grade and twenty times higher than the normal commercially used grade.

Wealth and transportation have allowed the global exploitation of materials, especially in combination with the huge mechanical lifting devices now available. This has encouraged the use of non-local materials and the loss of urban identity for many towns and cities.

Developments in the production process of materials such as carbon fibre have allowed much larger components to be produced on a much wider scale. Low-temperature-cure carbon-fibre materials that can be created at around 80 degrees centigrade avoid the need for expensive autoclaves. These can be formed in large heated plastic bags.

The development of form is starting to be limited by social issues rather than design values. The pressures on the supply of materials and their environmental impact are beginning to take a higher priority. At what world population or density does the *Blade Runner* system take over? Social legislation will need to take a stronger level of control over the development and construction of towns and cities. Severe rules will need to be applied during the second half of this century in order to enable society to be sensibly sustained and developed. The control of waste and its recycling will need to be a social priority.

At present, indirect social controls are influencing the construction of buildings. The influence is subtle but present. The universal lack of trade skills is resulting in many buildings being formed by unitized or prefabricated construction. This process should not be considered to be a negative one and helps to avoid many of the well-discussed and documented site problems.

The adoption of a structural material has always been influenced by the particular development phase for that substance. If a graph plots skill and material expression against time a common factor can be found: at the beginning of the use of a material the skill and expression level inevitably is low. It builds to a zenith and then wanes. If stone is considered, in prehistoric times its use generally was simplistic. In medieval times the level of material expression and manpower skill was at its zenith. The present use of stone is less expressive apart from a few cases and the manpower skill level is lower, with very few available operatives.

The use and development of timber shows a similar progression. However, the curve profiles of the future will be significantly controlled by the material's ability to be replaced and regrown and the energy consumed in its production or conversion.

5.14
Earth Centre Conference Centre, Doncaster, South Yorkshire, 2000 (architect: Bill Dunster Architects)

5.15
Trapion walls under construction

5.16
Completed trapion wall

The embodied carbon level of a material will start to influence its selection in a meaningful manner. The use and development of iron and steel rapidly grew during the Industrial Revolution and has now stabilized with modest growth. The potential for increased use of steel will be severely limited by energy use and environmental issues over the next fifty years.

In the Industrial Revolution Joseph Paxton developed systems during the construction of Crystal Palace to load test every cast component to ensure reliability of structural form. Some seventeen thousand components were cast, load tested and erected in seventeen weeks! This skill and resource level is not available today. As the need to use recycled materials increases, the load testing of materials will become more common and engineers will need to take a greater responsibility with regard to these issues.

Environmentally responsible and sustainable buildings are starting to be designed. Most are in their infancy. Some, when judged by today's standards, could be considered to be extreme in many areas. Some will be criticized for the types and use of materials with which they achieve their innovations. It is believed that most of these buildings will in time be seen favourably as useful stepping stones towards developing an appropriate response to new challenges.

The Earth Centre's new conference building in Doncaster, South Yorkshire, designed by Bill Dunster Architects and structurally engineered by MLDE, is seen in environmental and sustainable terms as a pivotal and important public building. The architectural form has been subservient to the functional requirements and evolved directly from them, which shows considerable skill and humility by the architect. Dunster's passion to deliver a building that is constructed from locally sourced recycled materials and that sensibly generates a large proportion of its own energy has driven the process. The design team created a novel and forward-thinking approach to the problems created by the client brief. Many of these had not been solved on such a scale before. The building uses about 75 per cent recycled materials and has been designed to generate about 60 per cent of its own energy needs.

The structure sits directly on 400 millimetres of structural insulation and is encapsulated within a similar thickness in walls and roof. The amount of embodied energy within the building fabric was to be limited. The foundations and a 500-cubic-metre concrete water tank below the main structure were constructed from low-energy concrete. The water tank is used as a thermal store for the summer sun's energy, which is reused during the winter months. Up to 90 per cent of the cement normally used in construction concrete was replaced with ground granulated blast furnace slag (GGBS), significantly reducing the embodied energy of the structure.

The load-bearing structural walls were made from recycled crushed concrete from a local colliery yard. These were formed into specially designed and patented gabion units called trapions. These were developed in conjunction with Roger Farmer of Tinsley Wire and have about half the embodied energy of a conventional gabion because of a significant reduction in the amount of wire used in their construction. The roof structure also uses large amounts of locally sourced recycled timbers. The amount of rework and subsequent waste produced was also limited, further minimizing the amount of embodied energy. The Earth Centre Conference Building is innovative on many levels and also creates a significant platform for intellectual and philosophical discussion.

The current market pressure to provide reliable, 'perfect' buildings does cause problems with traditionally crafted approaches. Natural materials, when used in construction, will always need some components to be replaced and repaired due to inherent defects. These problems will become more evident when recycled materials are used. But recycling will also create a new generation of standard and hybrid construction materials. These materials will form interesting and new challenges. A reborn and resurgent material is rammed earth which has been used for thousands of years in various forms such as clunch, Devon Bank and cob. Few things are new, just rediscovered.

There are not the mechanisms nor fee scales in place to deal with these aspects of tomorrow's brave new worlds. Additional pressures and responsibilities will be forced upon design teams. These must be discussed and agreed. The designers of tomorrow's buildings will be constrained by greater legislation and, given the nebula of 'new' materials, will face greater dilemmas. Will mankind continue to rise to its spiritual aspirations or become tied down by the practical considerations of life as the pressures rise?

As an engineer at the beginning of this new millennium, the changes to be faced will compound year by year. It seems that in the near future there will be a polarization of design into two distinct categories: low tech and highly intellectual or high tech and prescribed.

The selection of materials for schemes in the future will become more constrained by conscience and social influences. Most modern buildings still function on a primitive basis. This will now start to change rapidly. The Industrial Revolution brought many new materials to the palette of the designer and very creative projects were realized. I believe that the coming years will yield similar opportunities and challenges based on environmental grounds.

5.17
Earth Centre Conference Centre, Doncaster, South Yorkshire, 2000: entrance, internal view

Notes

1 A. Aalto, 'Influence of structures and materials on modern architecture', lecture given in Oslo, 1938.

Chapter 6

More than architecture:

David Marks and Julia Barfield, MarksBarfield Architects

Written by Dominique Poole

Innovative architecture is now recognized as a powerful catalyst for economic regeneration and revival of our towns and cities. Imbued with visual and aesthetic appeal, it can provide an iconic and symbolic role, attracting vast numbers of visitors, underpinning tourism, and becoming so familiar that it is recognized around the world as a symbol of a particular place. When allied to an inspiring concept and supported by a strong business case, innovative architecture can provide a tremendous boost to the economy, vibrancy, civic pride and attractiveness of a city or town. Vision, scale, but above all the quality of design, engineering and purpose are the most important factors in determining the success of innovative architecture.

David Marks, 2002

The architecture of David Marks and Julia Barfield evokes a strong relationship between architecture and engineering derived from a fascination with structure. This philosophy forms a common thread that informs all the projects they undertake. An example can be seen in their competition entry for a Bridge of the Future to span the Grand Canyon. The brief stipulated that the bridge should be linked with nature and this led Marks and Barfield to consider how nature would inform the design of a bridge and to investigate the biggest bridge that nature had ever designed. They sought inspiration for the solution in the spine of a dinosaur, leading to an investigation of how the spine functioned and accommodated the forces of compression and tension. The resulting Y-shaped component is similar to the bone of a herring fish.

Engineer Jane Wernick was involved in the design from the early stages and, although she was working in Los Angeles at the time, she managed to maintain communication via fax and telephone conversations – sometimes at strange times of the night. David and Julia would at times find themselves talking to Jane in her office in LA from their bed. There is a synergy between the three designers: Jane, like Julia and David, has always been fascinated by natural structures and is interested in the way nature designs. The book *On growth and form* by D'Arcy Thompson (Cambridge University Press, Cambridge, 1961) has been particularly influential in their architecture.

The structural principle derived from the dinosaur spine was also applied to a competition entry that won third place for a multi-purpose space as part of a sports and arts programme in Glasgow, where they added ribs to the spine to form a lightweight

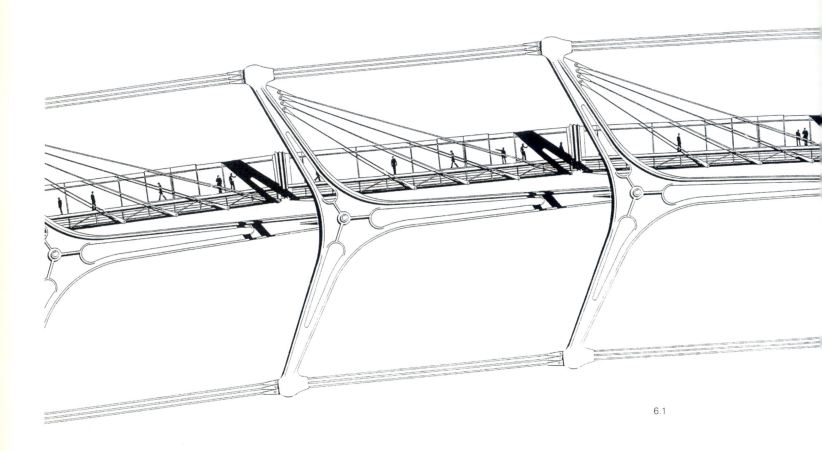

6.1

structure. This demonstrates a process often adopted by architects, whereby an innovative solution is applied and modified for subsequent projects – an incremental process of innovation. By gradually improving the idea the risk aspect is minimized. For example, if you look at the rim of the London Eye you can see its roots in the dinosaur bridge designed ten years earlier.

Both Julia and David undertook their architectural training at the Architectural Association, where they were students of Keith Critchlow, and during this time David became involved in building some geodesic domes for Beaulieu Motor Museum. Julia

and David took an alternative path away from the mainstream. In their final year, they found themselves part of a group that recognized they didn't fit in with any one unit, so they formed their own unit. It was a high-risk strategy because they chose a tutor from the technical department, which was an unusual choice at the time and led to some people actually failing the course.

After leaving the Architectural Association, but still working with the same group, they won an ideas competition but then struggled to obtain any architectural work and decided to form a model-making company. It was through this business

6.2

6.3

6.1
Competition entry for the Bridge of the Future, 1989, to span the Grand Canyon, with Y-shaped structure similar to the spine of a dinosaur (architect: MarksBarfield Architects)

6.2
Concepts from nature: growth and form as shown by D'Arcy Thompson

6.3
The rim of the Millennium Wheel, London, 2000, showing the influence of the dinosaur bridge designed ten years earlier (architect: MarksBarfield Architects)

6.4
Detail of the rim of the Millennium Wheel with the pods attached to its outer edge

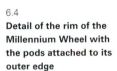

venture that they first met Jane Wernick. Julia became involved in a fascinating project for lightweight structures organized by Peter Rice. The company made a whole series of working models that demonstrated all the principles of lightweight structures, including a hanging net structure, a grid shell and a pneumatic structure. Peter Rice invited people from within Ove Arup and Partners from all over the world. Frei Otto gave a talk that Julia has described as 'inspirational – he was amazing, he had the enthusiasm of a child and the wisdom of an old man'. At the time Jane was working in Arup's lightweight structures unit in London very much under Peter Rice's wing, as his protégé.

Julia explained that by chance – one of those things in life that happen because you're in the right place at the right time – she rang up John Young of Richard Rogers Partnership (RRP) at a time when they needed model makers. David and Julia went into the office and established themselves as an offshoot of RRP, responsible for making their architectural models. RRP had just won the Lloyd's

Building job and David and Julia were kept busy making models mainly for this project until the Inmos Microprocessor Factory came into the office. They had discussed making the leap from model making into proper architecture and Julia approached Richard and asked if she could work on Inmos, to which he kindly agreed. Similarly David began working on Lloyd's with Chris Wilkinson, who was one of the team leaders at the time.

Lloyd's was a project that featured a great deal of innovation. David continued to work on the project for five years, eventually taking over when Chris Wilkinson he left to set up his own practice. When David himself came to leave, Richard kindly offered him part-time work, enabling him to make the transition to establishing his own practice. The experience gained through working for RRP was invaluable and they continue to be supportive. Often innovation occurs by incremental improvements as David explains:

> Architecture is one of those things that exists by reference to other things, always. You are never doing something absolutely for the first time; there is always a previous reference. It is an art unlike others because, although it is original, it is a bit like cooking in that you're using ingredients that other people are using as well. Very often you find serendipity where people come up with the same idea at the same time or at different times.

The London Eye

One of the London Eye's interesting but little publicized innovations lies in the entrepreneurial story of its realization. Like the World Sea Centre and Aquasphere projects, the wheel features Marks and Barfield's trademark integration of architecture and engineering but it also shares an entrepreneurial business approach. To realize the World Sea Centre and Aquasphere, Marks and Barfield formed a company, and with the help of David's father, they found a site, developed a business model to make the Sea Centre project a reality, sought investors and

6.5
Design for the Aquasphere project, which, although unbuilt, demonstrated Marks and Barfield's skill in making an entrepreneurial proposal, 1992 (architect: MarksBarfield Architects)

6.6
**Drawing of the
Aquasphere project, 1992**

6.7
**Raising the Millennium
Wheel, October 1999**

6.8
**The Millennium Wheel,
London, 2000: the pods –
glass was essential to
maximize views over
London**

raised £1 million in funding. Unfortunately the project remains unrealized, but the skills and experience they gained proved invaluable in their next scheme.

The London Eye's design evolved from a competition entry for a millennium landmark held by the *Sunday Times* and the Architectural Foundation. Although Marks and Barfield didn't win the competition – in fact none of the entries won – one of their colleagues, Edward Hutchison suggested they should go ahead anyway. Using the business skills and experience they had gained from the World Sea Centre project, and with the business modal already formed, the three of them set up another company. Because of their success raising funds for the Sea Centre they were confident they could again attract private-sector funding.

For the first eighteen months they funded the project with their own money, borrowing against their house. They also had generous help from Jane at Arup, who developed the engineering concept without pay. David and Julia spent most of their time and energy trying to raise enough money to proceed to the next stage. The *Evening Standard* provided them with amazing publicity after its planning journalist Mira Bar Hillel spotted the application for a 500-foot-high wheel. Intrigued, she went to see Marks and Barfield, liked the idea, and informed her editor, Stewart Steven, who launched the 'Back the Wheel Campaign'. Fortunately, computer-imaging techniques had come of age at exactly the right time, providing them with the technology to produce some spectacular pictures. They also found that if a newspaper was running an article about the millennium they would call Marks and Barfield for an image, so the wheel became more widely known. Then, through a chance encounter while delivering Christmas cards, the project came to the attention of Bob Ayling of BA. Six months later Marks and Barfield signed a deal whereby British Airways joined their company, taking hold of 50 per cent and providing a loan of £600,000. It was with that

£600,000 that MarksBarfield were able to employ Arup and others and carry out all the necessary studies to get their planning application approved.

Technically innovative architecture by its nature involves risk and uncertainty. However, David has explained that although they were always certain the project was technically achievable, there was one particular moment of uncertainty, well into the project, when they thought they'd lost all the funding. Their relationship with British Airways became difficult because the airline imposed severe restrictions on the way the project could be procured. The tendering process yielded a Japanese contractor who claimed to have a 'remarkable' solution and came in millions of pounds lower than anybody else. Everyone around the table was keen to accept this bid because it said exactly what they wanted to hear. However, three months later the contractor admitted that they couldn't realize the wheel within the budget, the specification or the timescale, and offered an alternative solution that took the form of a standard Ferris wheel. British Airways and Tussauds, who at that point had been selected but not appointed to act as the operator, were still keen to proceed but Marks and Barfield insisted on maintaining the original design and specification even though this put the funding at risk. Often, financial or management risks require stronger nerve than risk of technical innovation. This later when technical problems occured – for example, when the wheel wasn't raised successfully first time, or when the spindle was tested and the factory was hit by lightning – these were simply hurdles that could be overcome with a little ingenuity.

The whole 1,500-tonne mass of rim and capsules is supported by the spindle, a 25-metre-long cast-steel component on a cantilever 70 metres up in the air. Reliability was going to be an issue and, as there were no conventional codes to follow, the engineers had to rely on working from first principles to try to optimize the thickness of steel without compromising the performance. Julia has explained that there were many aspects of the project for which there were no building codes, as is the case for many innovative construction techniques because codes are often formulated from tried and tested schemes. The spindle was fabricated from seven sections of cast steel up to 300 millimetres thick and one rolled section, all welded together. How much it would bend and whether it would fracture were unknown. The only way to ensure safety was to test the spindle – a process that cost not far short of £1 million.

The testing took place in the Netherlands at Hollandia's works at Krimpen a/d Ijssel, where a giant jig was built. The spindle was surrounded by water-filled containers in case it exploded and testing was conducted at night, when it was safest. However, on the night in question there was an electrical storm and the workshop and equipment were struck by lightning, which hit the coil supplying the strain gauge so that the electronic measuring equipment exploded. The following day all the other testing data was collated and analysed and proved that the spindle was fine. The sort of bending experienced by the spindle during the testing tempered the steel so the process not only served to assure the architects that the spindle could endure a force far in excess of any it will ever experience in service but also helped to prevent any micro cracks developing into larger cracks. That was the dramatic birth of the spindle.

Structural engineer Jacques Berenbak has wonderful stories about the engineering design process, explaining exactly how the nodes work, the philosophy behind the forces and why there were all the cut-outs to avoid stress concentrations. The architects originally wanted to use cast-steel nodes because they are reliable and resistant to fatigue, but they would have been impossible to manufacture within the timescale. The solution they designed instead is both beautiful and effective. Jacques was brought in at an early stage with Hollandia, who provided construction advice to MarksBarfield before

the project was tendered, but had not been selected as the contractor. After visiting Hollandia in 1997 and seeing evidence of their work David had realized they weren't just engineers and steel fabricators; they were also builders of machines, which was exactly what was required.

The French company, Poma, were the subcontractors Marks and Barfield had selected for the capsule construction and, like Hollandia, they were brought in at an early stage in the design process. Like many aspects of the project, there was no real precedent for the capsules, and Poma were found only after much research, which involved looking at boat builders, coach builders and helicopter and car manufacturers. The architects went through a process of elimination, but no one company had the right combination of skills. Poma were identified and appeared to have the necessary skills, gained from the design and construction of ski lifts and ski gondolas, although they had never done anything similar before. One of the architects' first ideas involved the continuous movement of the wheel to conserve energy and allow people to move on and off as the wheel rotated. The combined expertise of Poma's people-moving technology and engineering expertise was ideal, although they had always used plastic rather than glass.

Hollandia also had the right combination of skills and technology. They had experience not only of large structures but also in large moving structures. Another important factor was the location of their works on the waterfront, which allowed for ease of transportation. A key issue for the project was that as many components as possible should be fabricated off site and transported in large sections to the site over water and eventually along the River Thames. Hollandia also demonstrated a willingness to become involved early in the design, which was particularly appreciated when the difficulties with the Japanese contractor arose in July 1998, only eighteen months before the immovable deadline of the millennium.

6.9
**General view across
the Thames**

Eventually British Airways were persuaded to alter their funding constraints. They had initially insisted on David obtaining non-recourse funding. This meant that David found himself going round the City explaining they had this fabulous project called the British Airways Millennium Wheel (as it was at that time), but that they could not take on the project risk. Julia has explained that it was like going round with both hands tied behind his back: if BA weren't prepared to take on any of the risk why should anyone else? But eventually BA changed their approach and took over the risk and the management of the project. A Japanese bank and a West German bank who had been interested in the project when David approached them then loaned the money to build it. By this stage it was 1998.

The funding documents were signed in October 1998 which meant they only had fifteen months to complete a project that should have taken at least two years. BA adopted a construction management route. They were really up against the clock but the fact that in principle they had Hollandia and Poma on board, who were both familiar with the project, meant that they could hit the ground running.

Glass was essential for the capsules because the wheel experience was primarily about the view out over London. This was different from the design of ski gondolas, where the view of the mountain is less important. Marks and Barfield were never convinced they could achieve the best optical clarity with plastics. There was also the issue of maintenance to consider; with frequent cleaning of the pods they feared that the plastic might scratch, reducing visibility, or even discolour over time. However, they were aware of the disadvantages of glass, including its significant weight and the difficulty in forming the material, but this gave rise to another of the project's innovations.

Marks and Barfield designed the pods with doubly curved surfaces to high tolerances that had never been achieved before. The ideal method of

forming the glass would have been to use ceramic moulds but this wasn't a viable option either in terms of money or time. Another nail-biting stage of the project ensued as the architects team travelled all over Europe to talk to people about how they could achieve the forming process. They spoke to Pilkington and a variety of other companies but in the end it was an Italian company that came up with the solution, which was to use steel moulds containing a sacrificial layer of glass that could then be re-melted. The sacrificial layer would absorb the unwanted parts of the process, such as pitting, while the real glass would be cast onto this layer. Usually when glass is formed the process is less controlled but the steel mould ensured a controlled shape was cast. The Italian manufacturers were identified through a great deal of searching, most of which was carried out by Nic Bailey, who was responsible for the capsule design, continuing until they were satisfied they had found the right solution.

Often architects aren't in a position to commit this level of time and resources but Marks and Barfield could maintain their involvement because they were part of the client organization as well as being the architects. At times BA wanted to sideline them completely; it was their money, they were going to make the decisions. But because the architects forged strong relationships with the engineers at Poma and Hollandia they retained great influence.

The process by which the Millennium Wheel evolved from a competition entry to the most innovative modern landmark in London suggests some of the complexities of the construction process. Often people were required to adapt or alter their usual role, as Julia Barfield describes: 'The whole process and the whole role of project management is changing – where does it start and where does it stop, when does the design start and stop. We were always pushing and pushing and pushing.'

Chapter 7

An engineer's perspective

Mike Cook, Buro Happold

Introduction

When I stop to think about the source and nature of architectural innovation I see a spectrum. At one extreme there is the profound innovation of thought in such people as Antonio Gaudí or Buckminster Fuller, whose approaches were based on fundamentally different ways of looking at the world. At the other end there is the detailed and rigorous innovation that, through research and small steps of progress, makes possible new, exciting projects like Mannheim Bundesgartenshau or the Great Court at the British Museum. To some extent conceptual innovation has been the domain of architects and detailed innovation that of engineers, but the picture is blurred and bigger leaps are made by people who do not fit easily into any such definitions.

I am a structural engineer and this must affect the way I see innovation. Engineers are given the tools for innovation but these alone do not create innovative design. Engineers hold a fundamental understanding of the physical laws that govern the behaviour of solids and fluids. They can turn this to the exploration of new ideas or to the confirmation or rearrangement of proven ideas. In the right environment this can lead to innovation, but there are aspects of the construction industry that discourage innovation and encourage repetition of the past. I

believe it is worth considering where innovation comes from and what encourages it because through innovation we are able to make the real advances that steer us towards our ever-changing goals and ultimately enhance people's lives.

From my own perspective, innovation requires confidence, persuasiveness, conviction and determination. It can be helped by what could be seen as 'misunderstanding' or at least a lack of appreciation of current conventions. It often comes when people are operating 'at the edge' of their discipline and see ways for cross-fertilization. Some of the great innovators have thrown away the rule book and invented their own frame of reference by which to work. Their innovation is completely natural within this new perspective and set of priorities. This is 'misunderstanding' on a big scale, but it often happens that in time conventional wisdom is superseded by the new way of thinking.

The forces against innovation in construction

Construction demands a great deal of collaborative working. Nothing can happen without some kind of relationship between a diverse set of people. Information has to be created and exchanged for it to be translated into action. It is easier to exchange information that is familiar than information that is new and unfamiliar. Many people in the chain may not be advantaged by innovation, so they will seek ways to revert to the norm. A contractor might seek to reduce uncertainty and risk in case it reflects on profit. A client might have good reason to err on the side of caution to reduce risk too. To carry through innovation, the architect and engineer must communicate well and with confidence. Models and well-articulated arguments all play a part in helping build up the confidence of the rest of the team. Clear expression of the simplicity and logic for innovation is essential. In view of this, communication methods and skills must be an essential part of the training of engineers and architects.

I find it fascinating and very instructive to note that many of the most innovative projects that Buro Happold have engineered are in Germany. This is a country where the checking system of the proof engineer would appear to be counter to innovation. The common 'proof' is to find a precedent; if it has been done before it is probably all right to do it again. Yet it seems that having this very clear system of checking generates confidence. There is a route, through testing and proving, that allows new ideas to be implemented. As a consequence, innovative projects do have a route of checks and assurances that provides a methodical approach to proving their validity. Innovative engineering is not just about inspiration; it requires methodical cutting away at risk through analysis, modelling, testing and proving. It helps if people have a structure in which to do this.

My perspective

As a schoolboy I was fascinated with bridges and motorways. The impact that they have – making new connections, changing geography and changing the landscape – seemed astonishing. They are constructive and destructive at the same time. When I read that the people who do this are called civil

engineers I decided that I wanted to be one.

Before going to university I took a year out and worked at Ove Arup and Partners. I struck lucky and found myself working in Ted Happold's section with Ian Liddell, Michael Dickson and all the future partners of Buro Happold. They were working on the Mannheim lattice grid shell for the Bundesgartenshau. It was a perfect introduction for a student. Here was some really innovative architecture and engineering. Everyone was learning on the job and yet Ted and Ian seemed supremely confident that they would make it work in the end. I was involved in helping test models of the grid shell to predict buckling failure, and testing samples of the connections. It felt like I was making a real contribution and everyone seemed to be having a good time – I certainly was.

It was a good thing for me that I had that period of inspiration before the 'perspiration' of Cambridge. The course in the 1970s was highly theoretical and did not really engage any creative spirit. But at least I knew that engineering of buildings could be exciting and challenging. Fortunately Ted and Ian didn't forget me either and when the Mannheim team set up a new practice in Bath they called me up and I became their office student for the summer. This led naturally enough to a position there when I graduated. Unexpectedly, Ted asked me to work with him up at the university, researching the field of pneumatic structures – again, an innovative field where we started by studying failures (of which there were plenty) and then developing better understanding of their structural performance. I was in a team with materials experts, wind experts and analytical experts and I learnt a lot about the hard slog that is research. Innovation in engineering requires rigour. I found it hard to jump from a world of being taught to a world of finding out for myself. Perhaps that helped me to see how hard it really is to innovate, and to admire those who can and do.

Those who can and do innovate

It is always worth thinking about the people that history shows us to have been great innovators in architecture and engineering. There are three that my experience and interest always bring to mind; three people who created buildings unlike any that had gone before.

Frei Otto

During these early years with Ted I was fortunate to be asked to help on projects where Frei Otto was a key creative driving force. I was exposed to someone who created his own frame of reference, which would drive his designs. It has always interested me that he was thought of as an engineer by architects and as an architect by engineers. This is a measure of the originality of his thinking and shows that he was working at the junction between disciplines rather than dead centre in one.

Frei has always shown a fascination with nature, natural forms and their origin – forms of greatest efficiency. This approach seems to lead to a synthesis of architecture and engineering born of nature. Produced in collaboration with other architects and engineers, buildings like Munich Olympic Stadium, Mannheim Bundesgartenshau and Jeddah Sports Centre are supremely efficient in their use of material and have forms that break free from normal architectural convention.

Physical models were always key to Frei's design process. These models were needed to generate the complex forms that would result from the natural equilibrium of physical forces. He used soap-film models to define minimal-surface tension structures, sprung-chain models to define cable-nets of equal stress, and hanging-chain models to generate the optimal forms for compression lattice structures. In each case the natural laws of physics were used to define natural equilibrium forms. Relying on the constraints of nature and gravity ensured that nature was respected. Our current computer-modelling tools

7.3 right
Soap-film model by Frei Otto

allow us to go beyond nature and create arbitrary, wilful forms. This can be turned to advantage (as with the Gateshead Music Centre roof described later) but it can result in muddled design with little technical or engineering logic.

7.4 far right
Antonio Gaudí's Sagrada Familia, Barcelona, 1883

Buckminster Fuller

Unlike an architectural education, an engineering education makes little or no time for study of the great engineers of the past. So I was pleased that, when asked to contribute to a television programme about Buckminster Fuller, I had to make some time to find out more about this highly original man.

The most striking thing for me is the way that Bucky's vision of the world was all-encompassing. He was not just an architect or just an engineer; his frame of reference was the whole world. His quest was to find ways of living and making things that were in harmony with the world, using material wisely and efficiently. Thinking and behaving in such a way, Bucky considered it possible for mankind to flourish on Earth forever.

Buckminster Fuller broke away from conventional boundaries and did not allow himself to be categorized into any particular discipline. Having his own frame of reference, he went about devising structures, vehicles and engineered objects that would live up to his vision. His structures were highly original – some of the most innovative buildings of the twentieth century and an inspiration to many great architects and engineers of today.

7.1 left, upper
Munich Olympic Stadium, with Behnisch and Partners, 1971: interior view

7.2 left, lower
Munich Olympic Stadium: detail

Antonio Gaudí

Having been fascinated by Frei Otto's approach to form finding for Mannheim, it was natural for me to want to know more about Gaudí, whose hanging-chain models pre-dated Frei's. Gaudí, architect of the Sagrada Familia and many other equally exciting buildings in and around Barcelona, has become one of the best-known and best-loved architects of the past. His break with convention and his willingness to explore totally original forms has captured people's imagination.

I think it is interesting that Gaudí was not an especially good student; he did not excel under the strict discipline of conventional architecture. Yet he

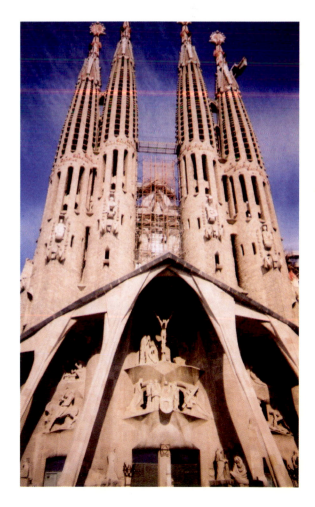

persevered. Being brought up surrounded by open country and having time on his hands through bouts of sickness he was able to study nature around him. He seems to have developed his own vision of how to create buildings as whole three-dimensional objects. Perhaps his rejection of two-dimensional drawn representation was an important part of this way of seeing and creating. He used physical models to find whole three-dimensional forms that matched his vision. These models became tools to define the geometry from which the masons could build. Being physical models they had to respond to natural forces (gravity in particular) and became 'shape optimizing'.

Gaudí had his own frame of reference; his own set of rules. Everything he created was judged within those new parameters. Fortunately for him, and us, he found a great supporter in Senior Güell, who financed many of his projects. This serves as a reminder of the powers of persuasion or influence that the innovator needs to have if ideas are to become a reality.

Thinking about these three great men of the twentieth century, I think it is important to see that their real innovation was in their original frame of reference. Everything was driven by their new way of thinking, a new set of priorities, a new driving force. Their innovation bore fruit because it turned its back on the conventional training and rules of the day. They crossed disciplines. They worked at the boundaries of disciplines rather than being subsumed in the conventions of any one. They had a passion for the world. Great innovation is born of new thinking and new ways of seeing. Sometimes it could be that this thinking is born of an ignorance or misunderstanding of the conventional – but that is the fascinating thing about it. Perhaps some of the greatest innovators have broken new ground because they didn't 'understand' what their teachers were saying! Perhaps too much of our training counters innovative thought and a little (creative) misunderstanding can be helpful.

Three projects, three approaches to construction and form

There are three relatively recent projects that I have been involved in that I think provide an interesting contrast. All have a degree of innovation in their design, yet each has responded in a different way to the material used and the means of construction. They serve as good illustrations of design that responds to circumstance, where innovation stems from a flexibility of response to the situation.

Mannheim Bundesgartenshau Multihalle

This major free-spanning hall stretched the boundaries of the efficient use of timber and the construction of a building of 'natural' form. It is, for me, an excellent example of the need for technical confidence in the engineering team. Ted Happold and Ian Liddell, the project leader, undertook with Frei Otto to solve problems that had not been faced or

resolved before. The innovation required a systematic identification of the problems and development of techniques for answering them. The form of the hall was intended to eliminate bending stresses in the timber grid shell under self-weight. An accurate catenary model made from fine hanging chains was needed to define the shell. Analysis of such a complex shape required a computer model of a scale that is commonplace now but was exceptional in 1973–4. To give a real appreciation of the level of risk of buckling of the shell, scale models were built and load-tested. Understanding of how the timber would bend and how the joints would resist slipping required full-scale testing. The way that the lattice grid shell was constructed on the ground as an equal grid of double timbers and then slowly hauled into position using forklift trucks was supremely simple and effective. The skin was a site-tailored PVC-coated membrane rarely used in construction, giving the translucency needed without the weight, cost or brittleness of glass.

The innovative vision was Frei Otto's, the innovating confidence was Ted Happold's and the innovative engineering capability and determination was Ian Liddell's – a remarkable team.

The roof of the Great Court at the British Museum

The new roof that covers the Great Court at the British Museum evolved over a period of about two years, during which period engineers and architects (Foster and Partners) collaborated intensively. The requirement was to cover the huge courtyard with a highly translucent roof without introducing visible columns and without imposing unacceptable loads on the surrounding walls. Many ways of doing this were explored until we all felt we had reached the best.

Defining the geometry was a challenge. The requirement was for a form that would rise between the outer rectangular perimeter of the court and the inner circle of the Reading Room, but there was no simple geometrical shape that would fit. The natural analogy was a soap film inflated between the

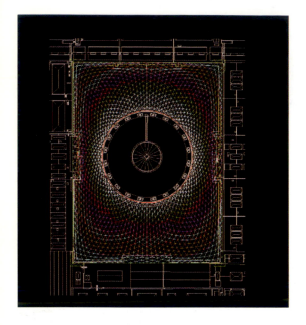

boundaries – it was possible to imagine a shape that would mould itself to the parameters. This was modelled on a computer with the soap film stretching into an equilibrium form much as if we had made a physical model. But this gave a form with too much bulge in some parts and too little in others. The way forward was a compromise where the 'memory' of the bubble form stayed but the shape was controlled by defining it analytically. By creating a three-way lattice of steel members that conformed to this doubly curved geometry we had a very light roof that acted as a shell and was highly efficient.

Typically for an innovative project, research was needed to build up the understanding and hence confidence to proceed. For instance, the node design and construction was critical. Fabricators were asked to develop their own approaches. The smooth roof form and three-way grillage of members meant that every component met a node at a different angle and orientation yet the connection had to achieve full strength. Research was needed to ensure that the weld strengths could be achieved in spite of the very considerable steel mass.

The innovation at the British Museum was not born of a new frame of reference. It was born of the determination of the client, the architect and the engineer to achieve the most elegant and appropriate solution to the problem. This was supported by the confidence of the team that it was possible to do things that had not been done before provided they were backed up by analysis, research and sound judgement.

Gateshead Music Centre

The new Music Centre at Gateshead comprises three distinct performance–teaching 'buildings' enveloped within a single enclosure. The architects, Foster and Partners, sought a form that would 'cling-wrap' these buildings and hence reflect their separate existence beneath. For economy it was important to keep the profile close to the buildings to minimize surface area.

With collaborative thinking between architect and engineer, the form evolved into a compression shell. To this extent it is similar to both the Mannheim and British Museum projects – all are

7.8
The Great Court at the British Museum, with Foster and Partners, 1994–2000: computer analysis of the roof by Buro Happold

7.9
The roof under construction

7.10
The roof under construction

7.11
Detail of node connection

7.12
The Sage Gateshead 2003: the roof under construction on the south bank of the Tyne (architect: Foster and Partners)

7.13
Detail of the complex roof structure comprising interlocking toroid forms

complex doubly curved forms. However, at Mannheim the form is created by bending timber beams into position on site and skewing the lattice to change lengths between nodes. This suits a flat site where the lattice can be assembled and raised. It also means accepting a degree of inaccuracy in the final form achieved – it better suits a membrane skin than metal or glass. At the British Museum fabrication geometry was complicated and required relatively specialist capability to construct. At Gateshead the freedom of the form had to be matched by extremely cost-effective construction. This demanded a very different approach to defining the form.

The geometry was strictly controlled using computer tools that defined a three-dimensional surface from parametric curves (circles in this case) swept through space. In one direction the roof curve was a spiral, defined by five circular arcs with tangential contact. In the other direction the roof was a series of alternately concave and convex circular arcs. The surface was formed from sweeping one set of arcs along the paths of the other. This tight control of geometry was combined with a deliberately simplistic approach to construction. The primary load-carrying elements are arcs that run across the roof within each valley. These are supported by inclined struts that reduce the spans and keep the primary member efficient and quite shallow. Between these primaries span secondary beams. Because of the regular geometry these beams are all singly curved to a constant radius (either concave or convex) and can be fabricated on conventional bending equipment. Tertiary members connect between these secondaries. These help stabilize the secondary members and, in conjunction with diagonal bracing, generate in-plane shear stiffness. This shear stiffness allows the whole roof to act, at least in part, as a shell, which improves overall stiffness and efficiency. The end result has much in common with the Mannheim and British

Museum roofs but it is achieved by more conventional construction.

The innovation in this case is the resolution of something that appears complex into relatively simple engineering through the tight control of form that computer generation allows. The design approach was original but construction is more conventional and can be undertaken by mainstream contractors.

Conclusion

There is innovation on a grand scale and on a fine scale. On the grand scale, innovation changes what is built through a change in the frame of reference of its design. This scale of innovation is most likely to come from people working and thinking 'at the edge' of their discipline. Typically, such people are hard to categorize as architect, engineer, biologist or philosopher. Then there is the finer-scale innovation that comes from confidence, determination and hard work. This requires people who are masters of their field, who move ideas forward in small steps using new tools or applying established techniques in new areas. Research, testing and methodical hard work is essential. One type is inspiration and the other perspiration. When both come together, as perhaps they did for Frei Otto and Ted Happold, things really happen.

Chapter 8

Touch the earth lightly

Richard Horden, Horden Cherry Lee

Written by Dominique Poole

Time, waypoints and *zwischen*

Creative time is elusive and sporadic. It is only apparent at times of great focus and mental relaxation. As with intense love, time disappears or speeds fast towards a moment when a couple are separated by deadline or emotion.

The creative process is like love, a full sense of being and of creation, the essence of life, it is the sole purpose of our existence. To pioneer and contribute to man's better existence on Earth or in space makes sense of the short time we have and becomes a legacy, an inspiration and a guide, a waypoint for others to help navigate their own innovations.

Innovation is not about big or small. It is allowing oneself the freedom to embark on a journey of exploration, enabling the mind to view the future as available, not inevitable. It is we who fashion our future, no one else.

Teaching and working with young people speeds the occasions for creativity. In a studio with sixty students all eager or anxious to move forward, the chemistry of innovation is always close. Properly to inspire and inform the young is itself an act of innovation and giving. Innovation is not about smartness or wealth; it is its own self, accessible to everyone.

One of the areas we find most productive as a basis for innovation is the 'in-between' or 'zwischen' in German – between land and water, earth and sky – and many of the most dynamic micro-architecture projects are born in this 'zwischen zone'.

Otl Aicher made great statements about innovation: 'Who designed the hammer?', 'Who designed the chair?' No one knows, nor does it matter. What matters is that they exist. The joy of the creator was his or her own at that distant time.

Richard Horden, 2002

Design philosophy

Richard Horden believes: 'Engineering without people is pointless, it only works if it is in some way useful.'[1] Although many associate Richard Horden with cutting-edge technology, he emphasizes that it is not the desire to utilize new technology that initiates the design process. He does not seek innovation for its own sake. His projects are informed more by an awareness of human reaction than by technology. They are born of a sincere consideration not only of adult sensibilities but also of young people and small children. This is not as common in architecture as it may seem. He observes that visitors are often surprised when they visit his office and he asks fundamental humanistic questions such as 'how do people relate to the scale of the building?' Journalists have a perception of a nuts-and-bolts approach to architecture derived from the well-known innovative solutions that Horden delivers, but what is often neglected or perhaps misunderstood is that his architecture is primarily driven by a sympathy, understanding and insight into human needs and preferences.

Although the appropriate solution may embrace technical innovation this innovation is a result of a youthful and essentially humanistic outlook. The fact that he so enjoys developing new designs with students is further proof of this. His natural sense of human scale has given birth to a proliferation of what he calls 'micro-architecture projects'. For him the future is in innovation by reduction and compaction, architectural information on a compressed scale, bringing people closer to materials, textures and surfaces and reducing volume, indulgence and extravagance.

The Courtyard and Yacht Houses

The Courtyard House in Poole, which he designed for his parents ten years prior to the more famous Yacht House and micro-scale Ski Haus, gives an insight into his approach. The ordered steel-frame design was inspired by the Californian Case Study House Program, a relatively formal, single-level architecture. It was built to accommodate his parents from their fifties into their mid-eighties and had to be entirely suitable to their lives on a practical level. His mother

is very artistic, a painter and opera singer; his father a lawyer. They were very tidy, ordered, immaculate; they loved to entertain people; they liked to present life in an ideal way, so the house also needed to be idealistic in its image. It was the first building that Horden designed as a student and was built out of care and consideration for his parents. His father stipulated that the house must cost no more than £24,000 and it was built precisely to budget.

By contrast, the Yacht House in the New Forest was designed for Horden's sister, who has a less formal personality, very human and very relaxed in comparison to his parents. So the architecture was similarly informal, consisting of a very light aluminium and modular frame system for ease of self-build. The project also needed to be extendable as Horden's sister ran a business from home. Its modular design responded to her personality in a loose and adaptable way. It is not a tidy building in any sense. The single module of 3.7 metres meant that she could build an additional room or rooms where needed while being aware of the incremental cost of each module.

Horden grew up close to Poole Harbour on the south coast of England. It was here that for many years he enjoyed sailing his Tornado catamaran, which, after use every summer, he could dismantle in around an hour by unbolting the components, packing them up and storing the boat away in its

8.1
The Tornado catamaran

8.2
Components of the Tornado

container for the winter months. The Tornado is a 9-metre-high, 3.3-metre-wide structure constructed from glass fibre, aluminium and stainless steel and requiring minimal maintenance. The rapid process of assembling the boat each year led him to question why the construction industry was not building in the same way. This produced a design for a new house based on similar principles – a structure that could be bolted together, extended by simply attaching more components, or dismantled and rebuilt on another site.

The special structural sections for the house were made by Proctor Masts, a company specializing in carbon fibre and aluminium yacht mast construction who were able to manufacture the sections more cheaply than alternative extruders, allowing a relatively modest budget for the house. The process of assembling the Tornado on the beach each year was aesthetically pleasant and its curved oval and round sections were light and tactile. The same sort of sections were used for the house because they were required to perform similar functions and because of their greater ease of handling in comparison to square sections. Although round sections are not unique to the yacht industry, the oval

section is made specifically for the industry because of its aerodynamic properties. An oval section is also relatively efficient as a beam, for example when used as a dinghy boom. Interestingly Horden's sister's husband also worked in the marine industry.

At this stage, in 1982, Horden was working more or less on his own, with an occasional assistant, Sarah Kirby, from his tiny garage in Hampstead. He was greatly influenced by the works of artist Polly Bins and sculptor Kenneth Snelson. He established his own office two years later.

Glasgow Wing Tower

Horden believes that 'One of the essential functions of architecture is to lift the human spirit.'[2] The Wing Tower was the winning and highly innovative design for an international competition for a Tower for Glasgow in 1993. Following Horden's typically humanist approach, the project was driven by a consideration of the needs of the people of Glasgow. The tower originated from an idea for a powerful symbol to inspire young people and the design was informed by Glasgow's shift away from

8.3
Glasgow Wing Tower, 1993

8.4
Glasgow Wing Tower, 1993: Peter Heppel testing the model in the wind tunnel

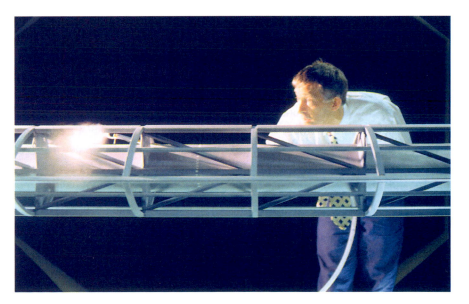

dimensions and slide in and out perfectly. While products have to be relatively lightweight they also have to withstand a 3G environment for several seconds at launch. Additionally, orientation is a very important factor; it is important to clearly define an up and a down.

Horden's team talked to NASA about BMW cars – highly ergonomic curved forms within and without – in relation to their work on the development of a personal astronaut compartment. If a rack module (measuring 1.2 x 2.4 x 1.2 metres and weighing 150 kilograms) fails it is necessary to manoeuvre it easily without damaging any of the surrounding experiments so the modules are arranged around a central square circulation area. The resulting design is organic in shape, defined by the organic shape of the body and its position. Astronauts sleep on the floor or wherever there is space to fix their head so the head restraint is the most important factor when sleeping in microgravity. Currently they use Velcro straps to secure their heads to a surface.

The Study Gallery

One of Horden's most successful recent projects in relation to young people, and one with a very human sense of scale, is the Study Gallery in Poole. The phrase Study Gallery was invented by Horden to clarify the new concept of a working gallery, a place to both create and exhibit art. 'Study' relates to the part of the gallery devoted to the study and creation of new works and to teaching. It is intended to make less formal the experience of learning about art for young primary school children, for whom the scale and dimension of the gallery is designed. The building is a prototype for many future, relatively low-cost, Study Galleries. The beautiful maritime pine in the courtyard has been protected and retained to evoke the tree as an early Greek teaching venue, to contrast with the precise cube form of the gallery and to express creativity in man and nature.

The building is a 13-metre cube, divided on the diagonal between a large volume for display and study spaces on three levels, which overlook the display space. Children's work, for example bamboo and paper mobiles, can be hoisted to a high level and illuminated to be visible from the street.

Richard Horden believes the relatively slow pace of progression of technical innovation can be attributed to thinking in relation to mass. Despite its modern appearance, the simple structure of the hang-glider, invented in the 1960s, could have been created in 3000 BC from a frame constructed from bamboo with a light silk covering. Theoretically the first hang-glider flight could have been made from the top of the pyramids but at that time mass was a thing of enormous symbolism and importance. Early architecture was more concerned with mass and compression than the tension and 'lightness'. Today, however, 'lightness' embodies Horden's fundamental approach to architecture – to touch the earth lightly, achieving more with less and minimizing the use of materials and resources.

8.14
The Study Gallery, Poole, 1994 (architect: Hordon Cherry Lee)

8.16
Hang-glider

8.15
The Study Gallery, Poole, 1994: illuminated

Notes

1   R. Horden, interview with the authors, 2000.

2   R. Horden, interview with the authors, 2000.

3   R. Horden (1999) *Architecture and teaching*, Basel: Birkhäuser, p.20.

4   K. Long (1999) 'Horden quits Glasgow Tower', *Building Design*, 11 June, p.3.

5   P. Drew (2000) *Utzon and the Sydney Opera House*, New South Wales: InSPIRE Press, p.5.

6   G. Dennis (2001) 'Architect disowns new Glasgow Tower design', *Sunday Times*, Scotland, 17 July.

7   R. Horden (1999) *Architecture and teaching*, Basel: Birkhäuser, p.98.

Chapter 9

Production processes, sources and the uses of materials

Eva Jiricna, Eva Jiricna Architects Limited

Written by Alan J. Brookes

Inventiveness is one of the most important qualities possessed by mankind. Without being inventive we would probably die of boredom. The architectural profession or occupation, with all its difficulties, has a very low risk of being boring or repetitive. Indeed it would require a great deal of 'inventiveness' to create an atmosphere of no interest, no tension, similar to one of those simple 'musts' in our life like brushing teeth or washing socks.

We have accepted generally that being inventive is one of those very familiar comments architects are striving for and architectural critics very often use to avoid making a positive statement concerning the aesthetics and real values of an architectural concept or a solution.

There is no limit to inventiveness either in ordinary life or in architecture. I am sure that there must be an inventive and creative approach to brushing one's teeth, just as much as there is a chance of coming up with a design for a new skyscraper in a shape and style we have never seen before. Yet there is inventiveness for the sake of it, whilst true

inventiveness makes a real difference to our lives and perception of the world we live in. The difference lies in the question we pose ourselves during the process: is it simply 'How can we do this or that differently?' Or, 'How can we contribute to doing this or that in order to make a difference, a real improvement to the final outcome (or to the way we make things)?'

Architecture, being such a competitive profession, and architects being so keen to impress, very often look for inspiration to other associated professions in order to come up with an application of different technologies, different materials, different methods of creating and building – for example the boat-building industry, space research and exploration, the aircraft industry and so on – but very often for only one reason: to distinguish themselves from the crowd. Even if the final results might be interesting or good-looking, they do not often reach any target other than new aesthetics, higher costs and the same, possibly very slightly improved, performance.

However, there are real inventive solutions

that occur as a result of a serious approach to the problem, which is detailed knowledge and understanding of the qualities lacking and possible difficulties of using the product.

Wherever the inspiration might have come from, there are brilliant ideas that suddenly occur and change history. It would be very nice to think that 'it just happens'; one day we might be struck with a ray of light and we will discover a new glimpse into the future. In my understanding – even if I do, to a certain extent, believe in those incredible chances in life – it is all a linear (or quadratic – who knows) function of the effort put into the problem. Strangely enough, lots of apples fall on peoples' heads yet only Newton got the hint. I wait at the bus stop every day with thousands of others but am never there enlightened by the theory of relativity developed by Einstein, who not only comprehended something very basic but managed to interpret everyday experience in a way that shook the solid ground under our feet.

There are little people who, with little improvements, make our lives better every day and every architect has a chance of doing the same. We all remember days when we had 'good ideas'. But we should also understand that every good idea stands on a foundation made of disappointments, frustrations, false hopes, or just hopes, and, above all, hours and hours of wasted – or fruitful – time and energy. It would be nice to believe that in the same way as nothing can ever truly disappear in the universe, all our efforts eventually turn into a good idea, a really inventive solution to be enjoyed by those who deserve it. What would we do without dreams…

Eva Jiricna, 2002

In his book *An engineer imagines* Peter Rice describes a classic case of international misunderstanding in the production of the cast *gerberettes* at the Pompidou Centre in Paris.[1] The tender had been written in French but made reference to a British standard. The German contractor found an equivalent German standard, assured that this was more rigorous than the French. But the contractor failed to understand the implications of the British standard, which had been developed to address the problems of making North Sea oil platforms and assumed a different behaviour for large thick sections than the German standard. As a result the first *gerberettes* failed under test. The situation was finally resolved by Professor Kussmaul at Stuttgart University Institute of Materials, who saved the pieces already made by reheating them. Peter Rice refers to communication as being 'the key to progress'.

A similar issue arose in the building of the Orangery at Prague Castle.[2] Here an exoskeletal, stainless-steel, tubular structure designed by structural engineers Teckniker (Matthew Wells) supports a laminated glass shell. Tubes are clamped top and bottom to the node end by plates designed to be held by a single countersunk screw. Glass panels hung beneath the diagonal grid are point-fixed by spider castings and silicone sealed.

9.1
The Orangery at Prague Castle, 1998: the exoskeletal structure (architect: Eva Jiricna Architects)

9.2
Royal Victoria Dock Bridge competition, London, 1991: node prototype

The structural node system was originally developed by Eva Jiricna with the engineer Nick Hanika from Price and Myers for the Royal Victoria Dock Bridge competition. A prototype of the node was created but the bridge was never realized. The design team for Prague proceeded with a degree of confidence, knowing the prototype node had been developed, and calculations by Teckniker showed that assumptions about node sizes and fixing using countersunk screws were correct. However, when the full-size development model was made by a Czech subsidiary of the German glazing company Seele, who also acted as manufacturers and contractor, the structure was shown not to be rigid.

Everyone was puzzled because the calculations were rechecked and found to be correct. Eva called on Ian Sinclair of Clifford Chapman Metal Works, with whom she had previously worked on her staircase designs. He was immediately able to point to a problem with the metric screws that were being used: there is a slight difference in the size of the Czech and British screws. Consequently no torque was being achieved between the screw and the structural component. Once this was realized the screws were changed and the construction proceeded to a satisfactory conclusion. The building

9.3
The Orangery at Prague Castle, 1998: prototype assembly

9.4

Engineers inspecting the development model

I am resigned to moving very slowly. British clients are very conservative and there is always an enormous time and cost penalty whenever anything involving new materials and methods is proposed. I have to ration myself to a small technological advance on each job.[4]

This sense of purpose and recognition that innovation requires careful testing is common to many of the architects and engineers in this book.

In 1957 Konrad Wachsmann wrote:

Human and aesthetic ideas will receive new impulses through the uncompromising application of contemporary knowledge and ability…The machine is the tool of our age. It is the cause of those effects through which social order manifests itself.[5]

Eva Jiricna represents a breed of European architects who identify themselves with those impulses. She realizes, however, that if architects wish to enlarge their constructional vocabulary they must relate to and engage in the industrial and manufacturing process. Without the support and knowledge of an industrial base, developments in technology cannot take place.

Eva has strong support both within her own office and from the manufacturers and contractors with whom she works. Partly this is due to the power of her own personality and kindness to others but also it is a reflection on her understanding of the value of advice from certain individuals within the building industry. It is surprising how often the names of a few key manufacturers and their technical representatives are mentioned in the offices we have visited as part of the preparation of this book. The architect involved in this type of work must communicate with and gain the trust of those involved in the manufacturing process, who maintain these specialist skills.

is now acclaimed for its light and elegant structure within its historical setting. The story reflects the rigour and attention required in any innovative design using principles or calculation methods that have not been proven over time.

To some extent Eva's commitment to her work may stem from the experience of her father, who was an architect. When Socialist Realism was introduced in the early 1950s, some architects joined the Communist Party and complied by taking instructions. Jiricna's father never joined the party and lost his job, working as a miner for a short period. Eventually he developed a career as an exhibition designer and built pavilions for fairs.

My father worked hard all his life but was not able to achieve anything apart from some national pavilions. He made me realize that I must stick to my principles whatever the circumstances. Unless one can develop at least one new idea in a problem it's not worth messing with; it's one's duty and responsibility to society to look forward, not back.[3]

Clearly Eva is obsessed by design but she often refers back to her interest in scientific discovery and the influence of forms in nature. She doesn't like to mix more than three or so materials or building techniques and learns from one project to another.

Notes

1 P. Rice (1994) *An engineer imagines*, London: Ellipsis.
2 C. Slessor (2000) 'Fragile state', *Architectural Review*, vol. 207, no. 1235, January, pp.38–41.
3 'Eva Jiricna in conversation with Alvin Boyarsky' (1987) *AA Files*, no. 15, Summer.
4 In M. Pawley, (1990) *Theory and design in the second machine age*, Oxford: Basil Blackwell Ltd.
5 K. Wachsmann (1961) *The turning point of building, structure and design*, New York: Reinhold Publishing Corp.

Chapter 10

Constructing the ephemeral – innovation in the use of glass

Luke Lowings, Carpenter/Lowings Architecture and Design

Introduction – why innovate?

The moment at which an 'innovation' occurs may be an impossible thing to define. Undoubtedly developments occur in technical methods that are notable advances, but our experience suggests that these changes are as much a product of a particular condition of society as the product of individual minds at specific moments. Technological innovation is related to broader conceptual, spatial and stylistic innovations – all are linked to the desires of society as a whole.

Architecture is an expression of the desires of a culture in the broadest possible sense, through

10.1
Munich Airport Tensegrity rings, 1993: the completed rings

clients, designers, contractors and producers. The financial pressures to conform, to continue using known solutions, make innovation to express ideas difficult and risky. Without the fundamental driving force of cultural goals the urge to innovate is confined to curiosity and the survival imperatives of greater efficiency and profit. Grappling with desire, and the communication of this struggle, is one of the roles of architecture as an art.

For example, one of the most ubiquitous of cultural goals in twentieth-century architecture is the notion of literal transparency. The equation of transparency with openness, freedom and a connection to 'nature' has been a major motivating force in modern architecture for eighty years or more, achieving the status of a rarely challenged doctrine, and is still frequently taken as self-evidently good. On a mundane level it has coincided with the development of frame buildings, relatively cheap fuel, the invention of the float process of glass production, and the need for a durable and reliable façade material. These factors have contributed to the general acceptance of the notion of transparency as a goal.

While accepting the positive aspects of transparency, we would like to propose that there is still a long way to go, not only to refine the idea but also to understand its limits. The possibilities inherent in glass and its relation to light have rarely been explored as a means of expressing other architectural and artistic goals. The potential for conceptual and visual 'innovation' is enormous.

The construction industry has to innovate technically at the same time that designers have to create conceptually and both sides have to understand and help each other if developments are to be possible. The work of James Carpenter Design Associates (JCDA) and Carpenter/Lowings has attempted to explore the expressive and technical possibilities of glass in parallel, and we have found that sometimes this is a relatively straightforward process and sometimes the reverse. Our work has taken place along the boundaries of the mainstream construction industry and the conditions that we have experienced have rarely been consistent with the disinterested professional role for which architects and designers sometimes strive. This has perhaps given us some insight into when and how technical 'innovation' is possible.

Of course spatial, perceptual or cultural 'innovation' is even more difficult to define and is in any event not an end in itself. One is striving for certain qualities in the work, but to claim that they represent innovation is difficult and to claim that they represent progress towards an agreed common goal is well beyond the remit of this article.

Conditions for innovation

The conditions that make a sympathetic environment for creative thinking on a conceptual and technical level are extremely important. It is difficult to be specific about the ideal conditions as every project is different, but it is possible and helpful to outline some of the conditions that we have found to be consistent in successful attempts to innovate:

- A clear concept (this relates to the cultural goals mentioned above but does not necessarily have to be 'cultural' in nature).

- A client with an understanding of, or at least support for, the goals that the designers set, as well as a willingness to trust and back those designers.
- Small groups (the design team and also the producers) with their own motivation and commitment to do something unusual. The companies involved do not need to be small but the groups need to be committed and cohesive.
- A design team (client, designer, engineer, fabricator, installer) whose members trust each other.
- Skilled and competent fabricators with the ability to be flexible, which usually means they are the type of fabricators who are about skills, not 'products'.
- One member of the design team willing and able to guide the project through to completion and willing to be responsible for the result – the importance of this cannot be overstated.
- An individual (or individuals) who can communicate the concept to the other design team members and who understands each role sufficiently well to know when they are (or are not) heading in the right direction.
- Nerve on the part of the coordinator and risk-taker.

The following are also helpful:
- A limited time-span or specific event that makes the end of the exceptional effort required visible. This keeps the goal in sight and prevents people focusing on the risk.
- A lack of structured design and control methods. Frequently the fact that installations can be classified as 'art' or are created for exhibitions means that they fall outside the normal procurement and control systems, so that innovation is less constrained and pre-existing solutions less likely to dominate.

Obviously some of these conditions are specific to

individual projects and some are more to do with the conditions of society as a whole. It is generally accepted that where there are many small expert companies there is more likely to be the competition and knowledge that breeds experimentation. There is no doubt a relationship between the profit margins of small, specialized companies involved in leisure pursuits (yachting and cycling for example) and their ability to involve themselves in potentially risky undertakings. But we have found that the improvisational skills of people with a strong craft tradition, where working with one's hands is respected and provides a stable form of employment over generations, are extremely important, not simply as a way of getting good quality workmanship but as an aid to thinking flexibly as a producer rather than as a consumer.

JCDA and Carpenter/Lowings have been in the position of having the right conditions on a number of projects that have had some quality of innovation. The technical advances on these projects were all in the service of a particular visual concept that demanded a better expression than the conventional method.

Tensegrity rings, Munich Airport

This project was intended as an artwork, one of several sponsored by large Bavarian companies to be in place at the opening of the new Munich Airport. We received the commission in late December 1992 and the airport was to open in May 1993 – a period of four months from conception to installation. We were very interested in the idea of using glass as a structural element to allow an appearance of delicacy and a greater expression of the qualities of light within the piece. At the time this was rare, especially using annealed glass, which has the advantage that it can be laminated and finished relatively easily.

Richard Kress from JCDA suggested using Buckminster Fuller's octet truss concept and it was agreed that we would adapt this idea, substituting coated glass for the compression struts in the tensegrity system. Two 7-metre-diameter rings of sixty-four equilateral glass triangles held by post-tensioned stainless-steel rods were proposed. Models and renderings were quickly produced and approved by the client. We were lucky enough to have the services of the engineer Tony Broomhead of Arup Associates in London, who had previously worked with JCDA on the development of a curtain wall using glass rods as compression elements. We could also call on the expertise of Art Wadzinski of Pilkington in Canada, who carried out detailed finite element analysis of the glass stresses under various conditions; Tim Eliassen and Michael Mulhern of TriPyramid Structures, who suggested the mechanics of a simple post-tensioning method and produced all the metal components, applying their background in yacht-rigging technology; and Depp Glass, who pushed their laminating, cutting and polishing skills to achieve the tolerances required. In addition, we had experienced installers in Brian Gulick and Gregg Morrell, craftsmen in wood and metal in their own right, and the German rigging team, who provided on-site skills. All of this was part of a collaborative approach to design that was able to draw out the best of everyone's abilities. Once detail design was complete, JCDA's role was to coordinate this team, making sure all parties knew what they had to do, designing the bearing pads and also simply organizing shipping, installation and client relations.

The post-tensioning method employed was to shorten the main radial connecting ties in the trusses, which had the effect of lengthening all the other connecting ties, thus compressing the glass. The amount of stress was estimated by calculating the amount that the rod would be shortened by turning a custom nut at one end of the rod.

There was no formal approval process as the piece was an artwork and was purchased directly by the client. We had no direct contact with building control and we did not produce a formal engineering report until after the piece was installed, though of course calculations had been made and analysed carefully in advance. The report was handed to the client as he handed over the final cheque. The clarity of the concept, the short time-span, the trust of the client, the availability of sufficient funds, and the formation of a team who were not constrained within their normal professional structures and who had developed a working method together in advance, allowed us to innovate in the use of structural annealed glass.

Macalester College, Minneapolis

We received a commission to produce a sculpture for a college in Minneapolis in 1998. There was sufficient time (though not a great deal of money) to explore the idea of laminating metal fittings into glass to increase the efficiency of the loading on the glass and to further reduce the fitting size. This would avoid the use of drilled and bolted connections,

10.2
Munich Airport Tensegrity rings, 1993: node showing compression fitting and tension rods

which concentrate the load excessively in annealed glass, as well as providing greater security for a two-ended glass strut in the event of breakage than would a structurally siliconed fitting such as those used in Munich. Engineer André Chaszar of Buro Happold in New York was interested in the idea. We again had TriPyramid and Depp to produce the metal and glass components, and were able to realize a complete structure using 2-metre glass struts and relatively tiny metal fittings.

The technical difficulty of laminating a load-bearing fitting into a three-layer-lamination centres on two issues. First there is the requirement that the metal fitting be exactly the same thickness as the centre

layer of glass, which is problematic because glass is not produced in perfectly consistent thicknesses and it may vary significantly within a single sheet. Second is the fact that there is normally some slippage between layers of glass in the laminating process and it is therefore difficult to place bearing pads between glass and metal in such a way that one can be sure they are taking the load in a controlled way.

For this project the metal fittings had to be reduced in thickness to match the glass and were in the end slightly too thin. The first time they were laminated into the glass they did not fully adhere and they had to be re-vacuum-bagged and put back into the autoclave at a higher temperature and pressure to drive out the air bubbles. In the end the glass was visibly distorted over the metal, but the fluidity of the PVB (Polyvinylbutyral) interlayer had filled the gaps and the pieces were usable.

The bearing pads were inserted between metal and glass before lamination and the whole assembly was held in place during the lamination process. There was a great deal of redundancy in the structure and therefore the piece had to be justified structurally in general terms only. We did not perform structural tests on the finished elements, but the end result was the first instance where we had been able truly to integrate the fixing with the glass itself. The compactness of the fitting and its small size relative to the structure itself were very pleasing.

Lens Ceiling, Federal Courthouse, Phoenix

The technical innovation in this project consisted of the use of a new stiffer and stronger interlayer intended for hurricane glazing, which was mechanically attached to a fitting. This allowed the use of much smaller and more discreet patch fittings than normal, which contributed to the delicacy and apparent weightlessness of the form.

The project required the creation of a ceiling for the main courtroom of the Federal Courthouse in Phoenix, Arizona, designed by Richard Meier's office in New York. Our relationship with Meier's office had been established through a number of previous collaborations, so our understanding with them was good. The Federal Arts Program officials saw the project as a testing ground for their official policy of fully integrating artworks into buildings. As with most artwork projects, the artist is considered responsible for design, fabrication and installation and, though this was the biggest project we had undertaken in this way and we were initially nervous because of the fixed budget and the inherent risks, we did in fact take the project all the way to completion.

Part of the concept was to use the central area

of the ceiling – a shallow spherical dish of rolled patterned glass attached to slender (12-millimetre-diameter) cables spanning the 30-metre courtroom – as a diffuser of natural and artificial light. This meant that it was important that the fittings be small and discreet, ruling out edge-supporting the glass in the central area where the cables converge. We did not want to use drilled glass because the fittings are large, complex and expensive so the idea of mechanically connecting the interlayer itself to the fitting was suggested. Two materials were tried: a PET (polyethylene teraphthalate) spall-shield film and the ionoplast interlayer that DuPont had recently been marketing as a component of a hurricane-proof safety glass. As designer, contractor and installer, we were able to get samples of both types made and test them under the guidance of our engineer, Matt King of Arup in New York. The ionoplast interlayer was extremely tough and able to withstand even the weight of a person after both panes were broken, while being connected only at the corners with a small bolt.

The fitting that we had designed supported only the upper sheet of glass, being set into the thickness of the lower sheet to keep the lower surface flush. We were therefore relying on the adhesion of the interlayer to keep up the lower sheet. Our tests were completely successful but as the product didn't have a history of use in practice we were somewhat concerned about the possibility of delamination of the lower sheet. DuPont's research scientists assured us that this couldn't occur. Incidentally, the use of the custom stainless-steel sprinkler pipes as part of the structure was an innovation made possible through the extremely un-bureaucratic approvals process of the Federal Authorities (and the remarkable fabrication skills of TriPyramid Structures again).

At schematic design stage we attempted to get cost estimates from one or two companies who might be capable of this kind of work but the estimates were much higher than the budget would allow and the only way to complete the project

10.8
Lens Ceiling, Phoenix: the soap bubble illustrates how the form of the ceiling is the intersection of a sphere and a horizontal surface

10.6
Diagram of deflections in the structure

10.7
Rendering

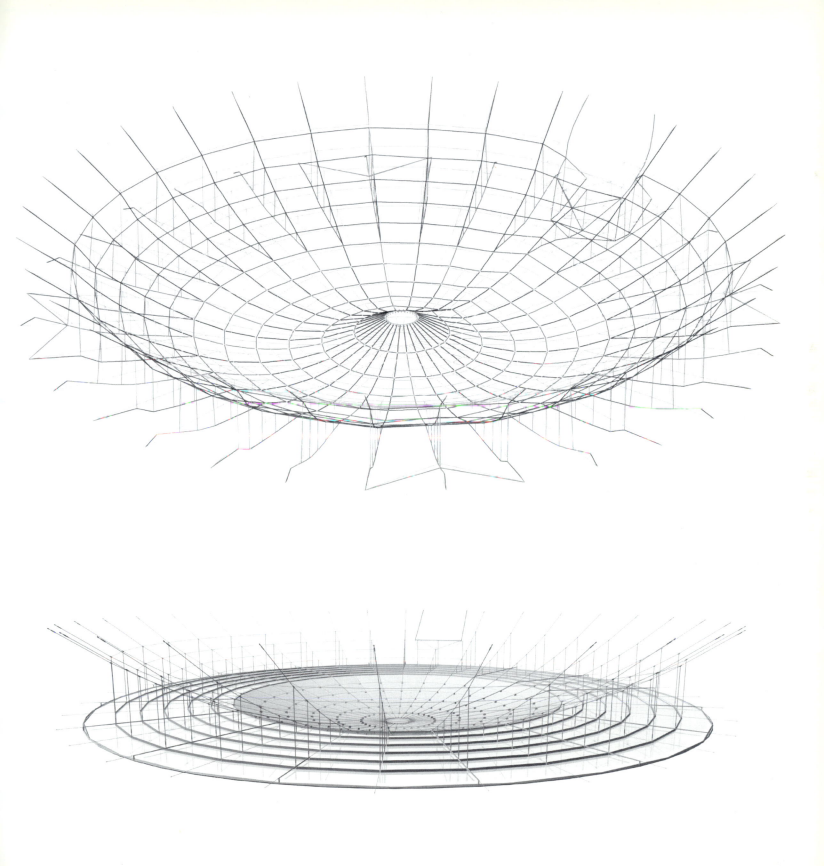

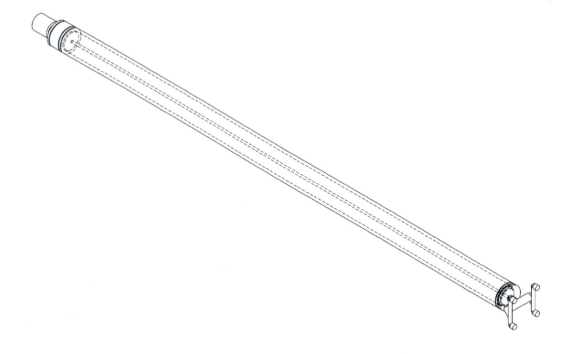

10.9
Glass Needle Field, Tower Place, London, 1998–2002: post-tensioned glass tube, early drawing

10.10
Rendering of glass tube field

within budget was to accept the contract ourselves. This is an example of an innovation that would have been extremely difficult to achieve within a conventional architectural professional structure.

Glass Needle Field, Tower Place, London

We were asked by Foster and Partners to produce proposals for the design of the public space at Tower Place, an office development in London. Part of the building design developed with Arup Façade Engineering involved a cable-net façade that was over 70 metres long and didn't reach the ground (the space behind was open to the public at all times). It therefore needed to be braced back to columns within the public atrium space. We proposed, as part of an overall approach to the design of the public space, that the façade's reflectivity be enhanced to reflect daylight into the shaded area of the atrium,

10.11
Resin lamination test samples

10.12
Two concentric glass tubes

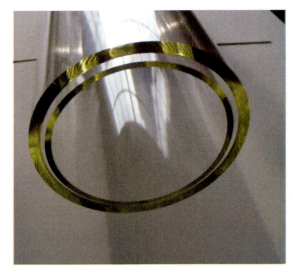

while the façade would be propped with coloured glass tubes, working with the reflectivity to create a field of colour defining the threshold of the space.

Foster accepted our suggestion in principle. But although glass tubes had been proposed as structural elements before, an acceptable method for making them safe had not been developed. We were aware that glass tubes in the diameters required were produced by two or three manufacturers worldwide for use in chemical plants and for chimney flues, but that only one was capable of producing them in the lengths required. We proposed a number of lamination solutions, including resin lamination, splitting one of the tubes to allow for contraction of the interlayer during lamination, and lining a single tube with a film. Tests of resin laminations produced for JCDA failed because of resin shrinkage, and without the resources to test our other suggestions we were unable to proceed alone.

The job was delayed due to a client change. When it re-started the whole of the public space was organized as a negotiated design-and-build package. The contractor, Biro Waagner, accepted the tubes as part of the design and were willing to write off the development costs as a public relations exercise. The

client also accepted the concept, provided that a design in steel was developed in parallel in case the glass tube tests didn't work, and provided the total cost was the same. The cost limitations eliminated the possibility of our further involvement, but Foster, Arups and the contractor proceeded with the idea, and the tubes – now unfortunately without colour – are to be installed using a split outer tube concept that has been very successful.

The glass tubes are innovative, but there is a cultural and societal context from which the idea sprang and without which they wouldn't have been built. The idea has a history going back to at least the 1930s and Giuseppe Terragni's Dante Memorial in Rome, and including JCDA's own proposal for a wall using chemically strengthened solid neodymium glass rods as structural elements, produced in 1989 for the Southern California Gas Company in Los Angeles. The work of Stefan Gose and Patrick Teuffel at the University of Stuttgart in 1996 that produced the Tensegrity Glass Cube for the Glasstec exhibition also pointed the way. The existing production facilities at the manufacturers, Schott, of course eliminated huge start-up costs for the production of the tubes that could have made the

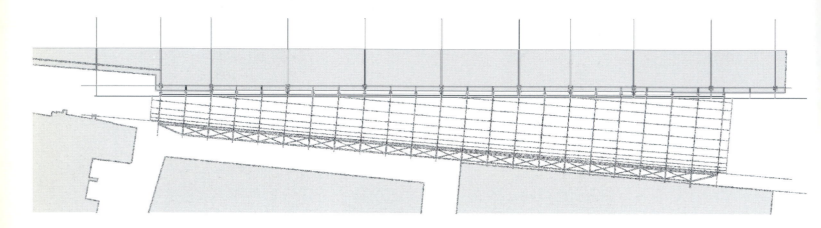

whole exercise academic. The willingness of Stefan Behling's team at Fosters and Arup Façade Engineering to resolve the technical issues of the lamination, and of the contractor and the client to back the concept, all contributed to what promises to be a successful conclusion.

Galleria, Plantation Place, London

The desire for transparency again became a generator of technical 'innovation' in this roof structure. We were asked by the architects Arup Associates of London to produce a design for a galleria between two large office buildings in the financial district of London. The design had to allow maximum possible visibility of a small church by Christopher Wren and Nicholas Hawksmoor at the end of a new public passage. Our concept included an asymmetrical glass vault that acknowledged the different scales and conditions on either side of the passage. To avoid using triangular glass panels with their concomitant large

fixings, we used a translational geometry developed by the engineers Schlaich Bergermann that meant we could use flat four-sided glass panels to produce a double-curved roof, creating a sweeping curved section. We also wanted to use the glass surface structurally, with no metal struts or bending members, again to maximize transparency. We developed a post-tensioned rod system that produced a stable vault using glass as the only compression element, working with Arup's in-house engineers (again including Tony Broomhead), Arup Façade Engineering, and the invaluable help and encouragement of Ben Fay, an independent engineer from the United States who had taken a personal academic interest in the concept.

Manufacturing tolerances to ensure predictable load transfer at connections, and a post-breakage strength for the glass that would allow the roof safely to lose a number of panels became the key technical issues to be resolved. For the first problem we proposed using a

10.13
Galleria, Plantation Place, London, 1998–2002: plan by JCDA Inc. (architect: Arup Associates)

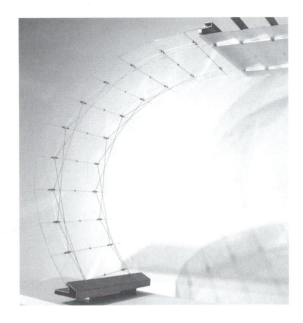

10.14
Partial sectional model of final proposal for roof and screen

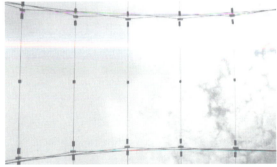

10.15
Looking up through the model of the final proposal for the roof

gunnable cementitious bearing compound that had been developed for masonry fixings and used on a number of projects in Austria, Germany and England in the last few years as a glass-bearing infill. To provide the post-breakage strength required we proposed using the same ionoplast interlayer that we had previously used in Phoenix. Preliminary calculations with the help of DuPont suggested that, given the correct bearing conditions and glass types, we could achieve the stability required even with all the sheets of a laminated panel broken. We had completed design development drawings when the client belatedly

realized that the planning authorities did not legally require the passage to be roofed and pulled out of the job, thus proving that active client commitment is one of the most important conditions for successful innovation. The conceptual and technical issues have in principle been resolved, however, and we await the next project to bring the 'innovations' to fruition and develop a true structural glass shell.

Summary

The most important aspect of a technical innovation is the visual or experiential idea that it helps to bring nearer to fruition. These projects have all had a visual idea of one sort or another that has been brought closer through a particular technical advance. But without the desire to make a better expression of a particular idea, technical innovation lacks a cultural and social purpose.

So, in conclusion, these examples make clear that 'innovation' is not an activity confined to a single individual, or even a particular practice or studio. It is a continuous dialogue between cultural goals – whether they are financial or artistic – and the means to produce things. The more flexible and diverse and committed to quality society is, the more likely it is that developments will see the light of day. Innovation is a relay race where the baton of the development of an idea is handed on over time and it is only when a concept is brought to a particularly refined or poignant or efficient resolution that the 'innovation' is recognized. To isolate one member of a team in situations such as this, or to isolate one moment, does not help us understand how innovation occurs.

Chapter 11

The tradition of the primitive with modern materials – an Australian perspective

Chris Clarke, Bligh Voller Nield

Introduction

Australian building technology does not generally experience innovation in the same manner as the advances in materials and assembly techniques seen in European countries. Despite cultural similarities, Australian technology caters to a smaller domestic market, lower levels of investment and government incentives for innovation, and a background of exporting primary products with 'value adding' carried out elsewhere. For example, zinc mined in Australia is sent to Germany, where Rhinezinc processes the basic ingots into sheet material complete with a patented pre-patina finish. Although primarily consumed by European markets, a small quantity is exported back to Australia for use on prestigious buildings requiring durable materials. This would represent the exception rather than the norm, as most building, roofing and cladding materials rarely carry warranties that exceed fifteen to twenty years.

A combination of low rents, short-term investment, depreciation through tax incentives and a boom-or-bust economy sees buildings going up fast. High-rise offices see one floor poured a week as a general rule of thumb. This emphasis on speed of construction and low building costs sees innovation in construction techniques rather than in architectural detailing and these innovations are generally linked to

exploiting the potential of new materials and building assembly systems.

There are exceptions of course, such as the early development of high-strength steels, resulting in thinner, stronger roofing and industrial cladding profiles prior to similar developments in other countries. Australian industry, however, seems to fail in taking up the full potential of such products in the way that Scandinavians such as Plannja have, providing longer spans and incorporating other properties such as acoustics by perforations to the web sections of complex structural profiles.

Australian building products developed mostly for industrial buildings have remained industrial in use and in product design. Architects are very good at exploiting materials and seeing potential in their application for other uses. But architects require the confidence and alliance of good clients, builders and subcontractors before innovations can be made on a building project, which may in turn act as a catalyst to further development and uses of the product.

The last and probably most important element necessary to encourage innovation is a direct link between client and architect, fostering invention and creativity within the confines of budget and programme. It is within the area of building procurement that

Australia has changed radically over the last twenty years, pursuing the various paths of design and construct, project management and construction management, which have resulted in a separation between client and architect. This is particularly the case in medium to large building projects.

Climate

Australia is a continent with a vast range of climatic conditions. From the humid tropical coastal regions of the north to the temperate and cooler south and the drier, more arid interior, considerable variations in temperature, rainfall and humidity occur. National building regulations do not include thermal insulation requirements or any focus on energy usage.

With this background the following projects are discussed as case studies of innovation. The two large projects focus on innovation in their roof design while the two smaller projects look at the buildings as a whole. The projects are more about a pioneering spirit than a sophisticated and refined approach to building design. They represent a personal list of projects in which myself and my practice have been recently involved.

Clarke Macleod House, Brisbane

This is a house I designed for myself and my partner, Jane MacLeod, in a leafy suburban 'backland' site in Brisbane, 7 kilometres from the city centre. The site was formed by a subdivision of land from another property, accessed along a narrow driveway behind a number of existing houses. It is bounded by eight adjacent properties, so careful planning to maintain privacy was one of the priorities of the design. Fortunately, in this part of Brisbane, which has the vegetation and fast growth typical of a subtropical climate, landscape can be used to great advantage to reduce visibility between neighbouring properties.

The house is oriented with an open and transparent external elevation facing north and a mostly opaque, straight elevation facing south. The 620-square-metre site has a cross-fall of about 4 metres, so a degree of cut and fill had to occur to fit the two-storey house comfortably on the site. The carport area to the north-west was set at a half level to ameliorate the steepness of the driveway and the difference in level through the site. The northern yard was then graded to provide a gently sloping grassy lawn in front of the house. A slab sitting on short-bored piers forms the ground platform for the steel frame. The link to the outside realm and the covered and welcoming 'veranda' space distinguishes the buildings from the fully enclosed European-style houses that still dominate the suburban landscape in Australia.

11.1
Clarke McLeod House, Brisbane, 2001: view from the east (architect: Chris Clarke)

11 2
The approach to the house

Budget and space

The house was built to a low budget of approximately AU$220,000 (UK£80,000), with a total covered area of 260 square metres. The aim was to design a house of modest area but with a generosity of vertical space so as to create a tranquil oasis for urban living. Another important factor was to provide approximately one-third of the covered area externally as a liveable veranda-like space. I had built a small weekend house for my brother beside the sea in the early 1990s and found that it was possible to build cheaply by keeping the design very simple and 'barn-like' as a structure. So in many respects the structure of this house was conceived as a simple braced frame like that found in agricultural buildings.

Steel frame

The Australian building industry is quite advanced in its production of steel products, which are pre-galvanized and generally used in industrial applications. Historically, this part of Australia was rich in hardwoods and developed a strong carpentry and joinery industry to accompany the design of lightweight timber houses. When I started as an architecture student in the late 1960s, this form of construction was the most economical and prevalent in domestic buildings. However, in recent times good hardwood has become more scarce and expensive to buy. In comparison, lightweight products made out of pre-galvanized steel strip – either roll-formed into planar shapes (purlins and channel sections) or pressed and robotically welded into tubular or circular form – have become more economical and lighter in weight than the timber required to do the same job. But these products are jointed and detailed by the building industry with crude industrial connections so another aim of this house was to develop simple and economical details more akin to the assembly of furniture than to the building industry.

I have been working on steel-frame buildings since 1974 when I went to work for John Winter in London. I became John's associate and with him designed several steel-framed houses and other small buildings. During this period I developed a strong interest in the planning and construction of Craig Ellwood's and Mies van der Rohe's buildings. Adrian Gale, who worked for Mies, shared our office space and I in turn shared in some of his experiences with the master. We always worked to low budgets but the fundamental qualities of steelwork, entailing precision in workmanship and overall strength-to-weight properties, resulted in fine buildings with minimal materials. The elegance of minimal structures combined with clear and simple details represents my intention in the construction and detailing of the Clarke McLeod house, as with all my projects.

11.3
Clarke McLeod House, Brisbane, 2001: beneath the catenary canopy in the veranda space

The Case Study Houses and Charles Eames

This house follows the key principles of the Californian Case Study House Program, whereby the beauty of the architecture is closely allied to the potential of current technology, workmanship and the repetition of details and assembly. The building is seen not as an end in itself but as a prototype for other houses. A project represents a learning curve for both the architect and the builder and it would be ideal to repeat these lessons on similar projects with the same builder.

I have always been seduced by many attributes of the Eames House, including its double-height volumes and its cheerful, informal arrangement of elements within a repetitive structural frame. Fortunately for Charles and Rae Eames, local industry produced a frame and panel system meant for industrial application that was used to great effect as the design tool for the modular arrangement of glass and fixed panels in their new house in 1948–9. Fifty years later I continue to work in a kindred spirit but because of the limited range of products available I generally have to design the frame and panel system from scratch, taking pre-finished components and having to detail fully their assembly system.

I share with John Winter and Frank Lloyd Wright a love of the horizontal that philosophically relates to the ability of strong, modern materials to span greater distances than traditional ones, as well as producing calm 'landscape' proportions that tie buildings to their surroundings. For me there is always a focus on 'the product' as a desirable outcome of design as well as a construction philosophy for the assembly of the parts. The 'big picture' is about creating a design concept for a house as both a spatial and a construction system. This then forms the discipline, like the beat in music, that orders the arrangement of the plan, the section and the elevational aspects of the design.

The frame and other building elements

A series of repetitive steel frames at 2.9-metre centres forms the basis of the support and delineation of the space. A 3-metre grid was chosen initially but the constraints of the site – including a 30-metre-tall eucalyptus tree together with a 2-metre planning setback to site boundaries – caused the grid to shrink marginally. The frame consists of 125-x-75-x-3-millimetre-thick pre-galvanized rectangular hollow sections (RHS) with internally bolted mitre joints. The intention was to cut the steelwork like picture frames with internal joining plates bolted through the walls of the RHS sections. These were developed with Greg Killen of Ove Arup and Partners, and we settled for a minor amount of internal welding, requiring some cold galvanizing (with rich zinc paint), which can be seen externally at the mitre joints. Exposed bolts are generally stainless-steel sockets, which look more refined than traditional hex-head bolts.

The frames are held together by the roof purlins and floor joists, which are galvanized steel top-hat sections simply tek screwed (without the need for cleats) to the primary frame members. They are 120 millimetres deep and are fixed at 450-millimetre centres as floor joists and 1,200-millimetre centres as roof purlins. To provide additional stiffness to the floors, each joist is lapped across each beam to increase its strength with double wall thickness. The floor is completed with particle-board, tongue-and-grooved panelling and the roof has a simple zincalume-coated corrugated-steel sheet fixed with tek screws into the purlins.

The entire frame assembly was carried out by two carpenters without cranes or expensive scaffold over about a week. The upper floor was laid in a day and the roof fixed, complete with fibreglass insulation, in three days. Before the frame was fully bolted and tightened the builder checked that the alignment of the steelwork was vertically, horizontally and diagonally true.

The carport roof consists of RHS outrigger beams suspended on stainless-steel cables back to the primary frame. The roof and ceiling purlins consist of cold-rolled steel channels normally used as bottom plates for stud walls. As these are marginally wider than the 76-millimetre RHS beams, I was able to cut sections of the web out of each purlin (the outer flanges remain intact), slide each member down over the outrigger beams and create an 'in-plane' structure rather than a thicker layered arrangement. The fixing of the roof and ceiling corrugated sheeting holds the frame together, making a diaphragm structure that is both efficient and elegant. The projecting roof sheeting forms a feathered edge, giving the roof a lightweight, floating feeling. The entire assembly falls by 20 millimetres to one end to enable roof and gutter drainage.

External wall structure

The north and east elevations are highly glazed and use a horizontal subframing system. The south and west walls are mostly sheeted with horizontal, mini-corrugated, zincalume-coated steel fixed to vertical steel studs.

The glazed elevations employ a series of parallel, 75-x-50, galvanized RHS rails, to which an aluminium

11.4
Clarke McLeod House, Brisbane, 2001: view of exposed structural frame and 'colonnade' to north elevation

11.5
**Living room with
perforated acoustic wall
and ceiling panels**

each rail on the main frame and drilling a hole in the outer face of each rail big enough to take a tek-screw extended drill bit. The screw can then be simply drilled and fixed through the rear face of the RHS rail to the main frame. A builders' clamp was used to hold each rail in place prior to fixing.

All of the glazing sections are square edged and slim in profile, resulting in a glazing solution that is almost flush with the outer surface of aluminium, which is anodized black. On each vertical face corresponding with the primary steel frame a pressed zincalume top-hat section 6 millimetres deep forms a shadow line joint that protects and visually coordinates the various cladding panels, which are also 6 millimetres thick. The mini-corrugated metal requires a bead of silicone to waterproof it rather than the profile foam filler blocks required for deeper corrugated sections and is better suited in scale to domestic construction than is traditional corrugated sheeting. Galvanized steel cross-bracing is incorporated into the solid panels within the plane of the studs. Timber studs are used in this instance because they are easier to notch around the rod bracing. On the east elevation behind fixed glass panels the bracing is exposed and constructed out of 6-millimetre stainless-steel yacht rigging.

All galvanized steel surfaces are left unpainted and in their raw state complement the pre-finished corrugated panels. These are silver zincalume externally and perforated colour-coated internally for acoustic purposes. The panels are fixed with Phillips-headed self-drill screws to top-hat battens or studs. The builder found it more efficient to pre-drill the panels on the floor prior to supporting and fixing them to wall and ceiling surfaces, pre-drilling several overlaid sheets at one time. Half the house (the living area) is finished with metal panels so no further painting or wet trades were necessary. By comparison the plasterboard walls and ceilings involved considerable mess and it took the owners a further six weekends to paint them.

glazing section is applied. This minimizes the cost of the aluminium components. Horizontal casement or 'hopper' windows fit within this system at high level, while 2.1-metre-high domestic-quality sliding doors are located at low level. The domestic sliding doors are cheaper than commercial quality doors and offer mosquito screens as part of the system.

The horizontal rail subframes are fixed to the main steel frame without cleats by simply overlaying

Staircase

The staircase is both innovative and economical. In this location a large K-brace between columns forms part of the primary wind bracing. The lower part of the K forms one of the stringers to the staircase. An identical member of 125-x-75 RHS forms the other string. Each stair is made by brake-pressing 1.2-millimetre-thick galvanized sheet into a V-section that sits on the slope of each stringer and is simply tek screwed to the stringer. A tread of 12-millimetre external plywood is fixed to the top of the V-shaped trays with countersunk (aircraft style) pop rivets at close centres, forming a type of stress-skin construction. The treads have a clear polyurethane finish and are used for storing bottles of wine. The triangular profile of each tread was developed to create an elegant and thin edge while also building enough overall thickness to minimize the open gap between treads, which could not exceed 125 millimetres under the local building code.

Stadium Australia, Sydney

Stadium Australia was the major stadium at the Sydney 2000 Olympic Games, used for the opening and closing ceremonies as well as for athletics during the games. The stadium was purpose-built but was designed to be modified after the Olympics for rugby league, rugby union and sporting events requiring a large seating capacity. It can also be used for major events such as pop concerts. The stadium seats 110,000 in Olympic mode; 30,000 temporary seats constructed at the north and south ends were removed after the Olympics to create a final seating capacity of 80,000 spectators. As part of these modifications the roof over the east and west stands will be continued over the north and south ends to complete the covering of the majority of spectator seats. In addition to the playing field and related areas, the building houses over 100,000 square metres of floor space over six levels, including club

facilities, dining areas, banquet rooms, offices and public concourses.

To give a sense of scale to the project, it would be possible to fit four Boeing 747 aircrafts side by side under the span of the main arch with plenty of room to spare. When I started work on the project I decided to draw a plan of the Great Pyramid at Cheops and superimposed it over the stadium. By coincidence it fits neatly in the square created by the four circular external ramp structures. Just like the ancient pyramids, the scale of the stadium is impressively heroic, and its completion in two-and-a-half years is a modern construction feat.

The roof

The roof covers an area of approximately 40,000 square metres with each long side providing 15,000 square metres of covered area. Structurally it consists of a giant curved space-frame suspended at its outer edge by a large triangulated truss. This truss, which is 14 metres at its deepest point, spans to pins in the concrete 'thrust blocks' at each end.

The design of buildings of this nature requires a close and inseparable relationship between structural engineering and architecture, with both disciplines constantly overlapping for all elements. The roof provides more than just rainwater protection to the seats below; it has to fulfil a range of functions, each requiring specialist consultants and contractor input. The issues involved include: overall design philosophy; structure; buildability; provision of a rainwater system; daylight; artificial light; and access and maintenance.

Overall design philosophy

The circular plan shape of the roof and stadium emanates from the diagram for achieving optimum sight lines from one corner of the playing field to the farthest diagonally opposite seat. As the stadium was primarily designed to suit Australian and international

11.6
Clarke McLeod House, Brisbane, 2001: staircase of folded galvanized sheet steel and ply top (stressed skin construction)

11.7
Stadium Australia, Sydney, 1999: view from the seating bowl (architect: HOK with Bligh Voller)

11.8
Thrust blocks

11.9
**Roof with polycarbonate
sheeting**

rugby football codes, where the best locations for seats are on the east and west sides, the plan was developed to provide maximum capacity on these sides with a smaller amount of seating at the north and south ends. To provide a concentration of better seats at about the halfway line it was natural to add greater depth to the plan in this area. This in turn results in a greater height to the upper seating tier, producing a rising and falling curve at the perimeter of the building. The three-dimensional shape of the roof reflects the shape of the seating bowl below. The high roofline of the east and west seating stands was reduced by sloping the roofs downward towards the playing field. By considering the height of a kicked ball and the line of sight across the playing field, an optimum curving line was derived for the front roofline. For both aesthetic and engineering reasons, a hyperbolic shape was derived for the roof, satisfying functional demands as well as the desire for a geometric logic to the structure.

A number of materials were investigated to cover the roof. Because the area of seats had such a deep plan, one of our aims was to provide a translucent roof; such a material would not only create a better seating environment but would also contribute to helping the grass grow on the playing field and would enhance television coverage of events.

We also wanted to collect the vast amount of rainwater that falls on the roof and store it to irrigate the playing field. Sydney won the right to host the Olympic Games for a number of reasons, one of which was its approach to sustainable design or 'the Green Games'. The use of the stadium roof as a rainwater collector contributed in part towards this philosophy.

Structure

A structural solution involving a long deep truss supporting the front edge of the roof and a hyperbolic space-frame grid was chosen because of its economy of materials as well as the overall architectural simplicity of the form. The main roofs span 286 metres between the high-strength pins in the thrust blocks and approximately 80 metres from the truss back to the rear perimeter beam at their deepest points. Circular in plan, the roof is subdivided into a 10-x-10 metre grid consisting of a series of straight lines in both plan and section that geometrically describe the hyperbolic roof form.

The space-frame structure deepens from the upper chord to approximately 4.8 metres at its mid-span point. This grid-shell roof consists of tubular members that vary in wall thickness to suit their strength and position in the structure. The 14-metre-high roof-edge truss consists of 1.2-metre-diameter members for the top and bottom chords. The roof hangs below the truss to allow for a separation of each element and easier waterproofing of the roof structure.

Roof purlins of galvanized box sections 300 millimetres deep span across each 10-metre bay to support the polycarbonate roof sheeting set into an aluminium frame. An economical roof purlin was developed with a specialist company (Stramit) who produced two cold-rolled C-channels that interlock to form the box shape. A 300-millimetre-deep RHS was not available locally and the cold-rolled solution proved to be very economical. We generally tried to use closed box sections for structural members so that the end result would be 'clean' and free of perches for birds to nest.

Of particular note is the detailing of the various brackets between the circular steel tubes and roof purlins. To enable the CHS (circular hollow section) tubes to be easily painted by an 'in-line' process, all projecting parts such as cleats or brackets were bolted on after the painting process ready for site assembly. This was one of many changes to the details that evolved from direct design discussions with the steel subcontractor.

Buildability

When designing a long-span structure 'buildability' is just as important as the theoretical design. Issues concerning transportation, cranage, temporary props, and pre-camber and construction tolerances must be considered by the architect and structural engineer. Steven Morley of SKM engineers, Multiplex, the main contractor, and National Engineering, the steel fabricator, developed an erection strategy in parallel with the design process.

Part of the structure and roof sheeting was developed as a prototype on site to test many of the details prior to erection of the main frame. National Engineering is a reasonably large steel fabricator but their works are located in the small country town of Young, about four hours drive west of Sydney. We flew there in a light aircraft several times to inspect the work, landing on a grass airstrip amongst orchards of cherry trees – Young is the 'Cherry Capital of Australia'. A complete section of the giant space-frame was erected in a steelyard and from a distance it towered above the town like a country church steeple. It was gratifying to see such a large steel structure created away from the usual big-city industrial environment, bringing considerable employment to a rural area.

It was our intent to minimize on-site welding so the majority of members were completely finished and painted prior to road transport to the site on the western side of Sydney. The main arch was constructed and assembled as three sections temporarily supported on massive steel towers. The two end portions were lifted into place first and surveyed into their final construction position. The central portion was lifted into position in the cool of the night so as to reduce its overall length and make the task of assembly possible. Unlike the space-frame roof structure, the main arch was welded on site, which makes for much neater node connections. The space-frame was assembled in cranable portions, complete with roof sheeting and

gutters. The world's largest mobile crane was used to erect the roof structure, the scale of which was, to say the least, inspiring.

The rainwater system

The roof panels drain into a network of stainless-steel box gutters on the 10-x-10-metre grid. The gutters, made from 3-millimetre-thick, grade 304 stainless steel, are joined end to end with white synthetic neoprene gasket material, which is screwed and siliconed to each gutter. They rest on brackets at 2.5-metre centres and do not require any additional substructure for support. The gutters also form the walking surfaces for repair or inspection of the roof.

When starting the roof design I found that the straight lines defining the hyperbolic shape from the centreline of the roof moving diagonally towards the far corners of each half circle were always on a fall and so could form a series of parallel gutters to carry the large quantities of water to the roof's outer edge. These are the primary gutters. By comparison the gutters in the other direction vary in fall depending upon their location in the roof. These were made into secondary gutters that are shallow in depth and carry the roof water a maximum of 10 metres before draining into the primary gutters, which are 300 millimetres deep. Both primary and secondary gutters are 500 millimetres wide so as to be suitable for walking on and carrying large volumes of water.

Within these dimensional parameters the gutters vary in geometry to suit the cross-fall of the roof, making U-shaped parallelograms. The huge amount of rainwater to be collected requires two parallel syphonic pipes under each roof and these work in unison with the suspended gantries that service the battery of lights for each roof. One pipe is located near the leading edge and the other halfway back up the roof. They are fed with water via a sump at each intersection between the suspended pipe and the primary gutter overhead. This pipe then runs via a

11.10
Stadium Australia, Sydney, 1999: syphonic drainage system

flexible joint to downpipes cast into the giant concrete thrust blocks. At the base of each thrust block, between its twisting concrete blade walls, is located a cavern, hydrodynamically shaped to slow the fast-flowing water before it is piped into four large storage tanks in the basement of the stadium. This water is then recycled to irrigate the playing field.

Daylight

Working with Tim Downey of the Lighting Design Partnership we were determined to create an even level of illumination on the spectators in the upper seating tier so as to produce an ideal background during television coverage. We also wanted to

reduce the impact of the contrast between light and the shadow cast by the roof on the playing field. This would also result in a reduction in the 'stopping down' of the television camera as it moved from the light of day into the shade of the roof. We discussed this proposal during the design period with television companies, who were delighted to find that we could significantly improve the performance of their equipment.

The even illumination under the roof was achieved by varying the translucency of the twin-wall polycarbonate material as it comes closer to the spectators at the back of the upper tier. The roof panels vary in translucency from 50 per cent clear at the front of the roof to 10 per cent at the rear.

Artificial illumination

For international television coverage of sports 2,000 lux of illumination is required and at Stadium Australia this is provided by a battery of lights in two rows under the roof. With a large stadium and a relatively high roof it is possible to avoid the use of lighting towers in providing good illumination on the pitch. The roof-level lights are masked and shaded by the roof so that unwanted light does not spread into the surrounding neighbourhood. Gantries located within the depth of the space-frame support all the sporting lights as well as providing access to the roof. These required considerable three-dimensional modelling to determine their layout.

Ansett Domestic Airlines Terminal, Sydney

The Ansett Terminal Building was completed for the Sydney 2000 Olympic Games, design having started rather late to meet an opening date of January 2000. The new two-storey terminal replaced an existing collection of single-storey buildings, including an aircraft hangar from the 1930s. It had to coordinate with the construction by the Sydney Airport Corporation of a two-level ring road around the entire domestic terminal area. The road enabled the vertical separation of departing and arriving passengers – the traditional arrangement for many larger airports.

The late start to the project and the immovable completion date prompted the design team to create a prefabricated series of building elements for fast erection on site. The project was also designed and constructed around the continuing operation of the existing terminal, which functioned 365 days a year and 18 hours a day. This was probably the most difficult factor to contend with and was made possible only by dividing the project into carefully orchestrated stages whereby each part was demolished and reconstructed in sequence.

The building is linear with long glass elevations facing north and south. Construction started in the east in the valet car-parking area and quickly moved westwards to create the departure check-in area at the upper level and a new arrival and baggage-handling area at ground level.

The roof was formed of a series of prefabricated shell truss elements supported on tripod steel columns. The structure is clearly expressed and contributes greatly to the architecture in both form and detail, representing a fusion of the functions and requirements of architecture and engineering within one building element.

11.11
Ansett Domestic Airlines Terminal, Sydney, 2000: exterior view with elevated road (architect: Bligh Voller Nield)

The roof

The gently sloping roof at 3 degrees tilts up to face the south, creating a greater glass area with views to Botany Bay. The north façade is lower and more shaded, as this is the sunny side of the building in the Southern Hemisphere. The roof has a largely clear span of 40 metres between façades and projects a further 3 metres past the tilted glass walls to create shade and suggest a floating appearance. The body of the shell truss is located within the enclosed building area, while its flat top cantilevers out to form projecting eaves. The building is designed as a series of 12-metre-wide modules and the roof relates to this module. Each roof element is approximately 11 metres wide with a 1-metre-wide light separating the shell trusses. The clear separation of the trusses allowed the elements to be separately prefabricated.

We resolved in early discussions with the engineer, Connell Wagner, two strategies to keep the trusses economical and easy to build. The word 'truss' was deliberately included in the name as this is considered a 'normal' building term for an economical and easily comprehensible structural item. Trusses are usually planar or prismatic but in this case the truss is an inverted barrel vault which may have been perceived as unusual and therefore expensive to build. Our intention was to create the perception of simplicity through semantics. At this time, when a considerable amount of steelwork was being fabricated for Olympic projects, steel contractors were busy and could tailor their prices to suit the job.

Our other strategy to ensure that the shell truss was economical and easy to build involved as much repetition as possible in member sizes, lengths and connections. We selected an inverted T-shape so that the ceiling panels of corrugated metal could sit in the flanges of the T. Straightforward and unrefined bolted connections occur in the web of the T out of sight above the ceiling line.

We intended to build the ceiling from perforated and corrugated steel sheet. However, when the builder was appointed he chose to have the ceilings rolled out of aluminium, which is lighter and easier to lift. External aircraft noise is minimized by the large air gap in the hollow truss in combination with the roof and ceiling sheeting. Our acoustic consultants pointed out that more noise is usually generated internally than externally in airport terminals, so a considerable amount of absorption was required in the ceiling surfaces.

Construction

The steel structure, consisting entirely of repetitive off-the-peg steel members, was prepared in the steel subcontractors works. Each truss was assembled for checking, then unbolted to a manageable size for transportation to the site. On site the pieces were assembled on the upper concrete deck on a series of slightly elevated supports so that the shell structure was accessible from above and below for the various trades.

Each lattice-like structure was completed with both a metal roof deck and corrugated aluminium ceiling panels prior to erection. Services such as lighting, sprinklers and smoke-extractor fans were installed before the entire assembly was lifted into position and propped up by the tripod steel columns. A temporary A-frame gantry was constructed to lift each truss into position. After the initial learning curve, trusses were constructed on a ten-day cycle.

Each tripod column consisted of a welded flat plate making a three-sided, triangular structure, which, because of its geometric form, was more easily joined at the base than a circular tubular structure. These angular forms take on a sculptural quality and as a series of repetitive elements have a strong and delightful appearance in the space of the check-in hall. The check-in hall interior has been used extensively in television advertising with the roof structure and tripod columns making an important contribution to the image of a modern airport terminal.

11.12
Tripod columns and shell-truss roof

11.13
Walk-through check-in counters with tripod columns

Sunshine Coast University Innovation Centre

The Innovation Centre at the entrance to the Sunshine Coast University houses several functions under one oversailing roof. Located 100 kilometres north of Brisbane, this is a new university campus and the client recognizes the importance of good architecture working in parallel with academic prowess. The Vice-Chancellor has encouraged the use of reputed architects and, unlike officials at several other universities in Queensland, he and his facilities manager have followed a traditional tendering process to achieve both quality and value for money.

The Innovation Centre contains three primary functions within its largely triangular-plan form. The widest part of the building forms a large assembly space that can be subdivided by three movable partitions for smaller groups. Up to 2,000 people can assemble there for graduation ceremonies or musical performances, and the space can also house exhibitions and conferences. The expanding plan shape opens out to face the remainder of the campus over a wide grassy plain where kangaroos graze. This is the only part of the building that is air-conditioned.

A narrow 'breezeway' separates the main hall from a teaching area that adjoins a series of similar rooms around an atrium space. In this area small office spaces house fledgling businesses that share knowledge and use the resources of the university. As these activities grow, the accommodation will expand into the current language school, which will be relocated. This is the 'innovation' end of the facilities that gives its name to the building.

The project began as a design think-tank held on the campus over several days when the design team (architect, engineers and quantity surveyor) participated in a workshop session with the university staff to understand their requirements and produce optional concept designs before honing in on the preferred option. As a design process this forged a bond between the users and the design team as well as showing the way forward in a

remarkably short period of time. Good buildings tend to grow out of a process where the client plays a significant role within the design team and nurtures the creative process. This project typifies this approach.

One building

The option to create two separate buildings was seriously explored. However, the strong presence of a single building sitting long and low in the open landscape soon became the preferred option. The teaching and business accommodation could be laid out over two storeys, matching the height of the hall, with the rooms arranged around small atrium spaces containing communal services such as photocopying, kitchens and lounges.

One roof

The various functions were focused beneath one roof and this was developed as a torroid shape so as to enclose the maximum area within the minimum height to reduce the cost of external wall cladding.

11.14
Sunshine Coast University Innovation Centre, Queensland Australia, 2001: view along the colonnade with thermal chimneys (architect: Bligh Voller Nield)

The difficulty of constructing a waterproof, metal deck roof with minimum pitch over such a long length lay in the detailing and construction of the joints to the roof sheeting. A membrane roof is not an option for a low-cost building in Australia as the technology is not well known within the building industry and the high intensity of ultraviolet light would affect the life of typical membrane material.

The metal deck roof comprises wide trays approximately 40 millimetres deep that can carry large quantities of rainwater, allowing for 350 millimetres rainfall in one hour, a storm intensity that in theory occurs once in every hundred years. By comparison in the UK rainfall intensity is 75 millimetres in one hour. Typically the length of each sheet is affected by road transport, which can only carry a maximum of 25 metres in length. Each tray overlaps the adjacent one and is held to the roof purlins by clips that permit the roof material to move longitudinally for expansion and contraction.

The overlapping roof joints form a key detail, permitting thermal movement of the roof while keeping out rainwater. In this instance on the upper part of the roof the pitch had to be a minimum of 1 degree at the upper expansion joint. As a precaution we added an internal gutter under the joint in case any rain penetration occurred. This has proven to be a wise addition as wind-driven rain has on occasion been carried upwards through the overlapping joint to be caught by the underlying gutter, which drains at each end over the wall cladding.

The thermal chimneys

Most recent passive design measures in architecture have been carried out in Europe and in colder climates where legislation, energy costs and a responsible political climate have encouraged green design. In Australia, where energy is still comparatively cheap and where architecture and building procurement is led largely by conservative construction companies,

serious examples of passive design are rare. It was decided to pursue a passive ventilation system for the Innovation Centre as part of a 'no air-conditioning' policy for the campus. The ventilation design, under the specialist guidance of Che Wall at Advanced Environmental Concepts, was studied from first principles working with computer simulation.

The thermal chimneys work in conjunction with the atrium spaces and voids above the suspended ceilings to draw air in from openable external windows. They are clad in translucent fibreglass with open upper areas to discharge the warm air. The chimneys heat up through solar radiation, causing warm air to rise and be expelled out through the protective overhanging roof. This in turn draws up the air from below to create ventilation through the deeper parts of the office and atrium spaces. Care

11.15
Atrium with thermal chimney

was taken in the design to provide sufficient overhang to reduce the possibility of wind-driven rain entering the solar chimneys. At the base of each chimney are electrically openable louvre grilles that remain closed until the air above is sufficiently buoyant to create the desired movement of air. These louvres also prevent a reverse movement of air in the cooler evening period. The thermal chimneys also act as roof lights to the atrium spaces. At night they light up like lanterns above the dark rooftop providing an impressive architectural feature to signpost the Innovation Centre.

We were careful not to place the chimneys or any other roof penetrations at the flattest part of the roof where they might cause leaks. The chimney roofs drain separately from the main roof to minimize the impact of the rainwater discharged into the adjacent roof trays.

Elevations

The orientation of the Innovation Centre relates to the major axis of the campus, which runs from the south-east to the north-west. As a result each elevation has a different relation to the path of the sun and is designed accordingly to minimize the impact of solar radiation.

A deeply projecting roof to the north-east shelters a colonnade and the entrance to all the building's facilities. A series of horizontal sunshading blades are connected to the external steel columns, growing in number as the roof slowly rises in curvature. The blades are made from Z-section purlins with additional perforations to dapple the sunlight penetrating into the colonnade. The narrow north-western end features an oversailing roof and large, vertical, perforated metal louvres to reduce the impact of the hot afternoon sun. The long south-western elevation is flush with the roof and comprises long, horizontal windows protected by angled sunshades and vertical fins. Sunshades and external cladding are all made from silver-zincalume-coated corrugated steel sheeting – one of the cheapest building materials available.

The end result is, however, anything but 'cheap', proving that through careful detailing and discipline in the number of materials used, good design and great architecture can still be achieved.

11.16
Sunshine Coast University Innovation Centre: cladding and sunshading

Chapter 12

A passion for building

Volkwin Marg, Architeckten von Gerkan, Marg & Partners

Written by Alan J. Brookes

Our aim is to design things as simply as possible, so that they have content and durability. Formal modesty and material unity is based on this assumption, because we believe that purposefulness is a categorical imperative. We wish to design a building simply, naturally and sensibly, to create space and enclosure that is as permanent as possible with low maintenance for the variety of human existence. We try to avoid expressionistic shapes, derived only from artistic whimsy without any consideration of nature, construction and wear through use, by questioning our own work and adopting a critical distance from topical architectural motives.

Volkwin Marg, 1995

Von Gerkan, Marg and Partners are one of the most innovative and prolific architectural offices in Germany. In the past thirty years they have planned and constructed buildings in most German cities, including Stuttgart and Hamburg airports. They have designed small-scale homes, the interiors of German high-speed trains, hotels, theatres, concert halls, office buildings, commercial centres, hospitals and research facilities.

Although clearly dynamic, Volkwin Marg remains a modest man who cares for his students at Aachen and has as a strong interest away from the office: his three-masted Baltic schooner, the *Activ*, which he converted himself from its original role as a cargo boat.

From his office in Hamburg he looks down on the cranes at the docks and on a tugboat that he also owns. It is therefore not surprising to learn that since childhood – he was born in 1936 in Königsberg and grew up in Danzig – he has taken a keen interest in boats and the natural materials used in their construction. After fleeing to the West in 1956 he joined his future partner, Meinhard von Gerkan, in studying architecture in Berlin and Brunswick.

His passion for sailing boats and the balance between the power of the wind in the sails and the tension of the rigging is obvious. But although he and Richard Horden share this interest, Marg's is not concerned with high-tech rigging and aluminium but leans more towards the traditional materials of sails and ropes and the movement and resulting sound of the wooden decking. He chose the trees used for the masts on the *Activ*, looking particularly for the straightest trunks and those free of knots.

The architecture of Von Gerkan, Marg and Partners is identified with their use of glass and steel at the new trade fair building at Leipzig and the Hamburg Museum of Local History, where a delicate arrangement of steel and glass with three spider-like

12.1
The Pavilion of Christian Religions at the Hanover Trade Fair, 2000: glazed infill panel

12.3
Hanover Trade Fair Hall, 2000: glass ducts for air circulation

12.2 left
Hanover Trade Fair Hall, 2000: double-layered façade (architect: Von Gerkan Marg and Partners)

trusses supports a curvilinear glazed roof.[1] But the practice retains its involvement in the textural use of materials, as clearly displayed in the infill panels of the Pavilion of Christian Religions at the Hanover Trade Fair with its amazing combination of poppies, strings, coal, tea strainers and so on, set within the inner space of double-glazed units.[2] As Toshio Nakamura writes in *The Architecture of Von Gerkan, Marg & Partners*: 'Texture is an immeasurable entity. It is a nuance, a touch, a haptic quality with an innate sense of ambiguity.'[3]

Marg admits to the early influence of Hans Scharoun and Modern Movement architects and their use of symbolism to relate the style of ships to new forms of architecture to represent a modern image. Clearly this imagery was present in the master structure supporting the log Menschliche

Messe at the Leipzig Fair. Designed in collaboration with the engineers Schlaich, Bergermann and Partners, with whom Marg has a close working relationship, this structure reflects the pragmatic design of a rigged and masted structure, influenced by tall ships. It is the close relationship they have with these engineers that distinguishes von Gerkan and Marg from other German practices. In this respect they are similar to Wilkinson Eyre in the UK, who work closely with engineers such as Tony Hunt and Ove Arup and Partners. Within the office Marg's younger partner, Hubert Nienhoff, and project leader Mark Ziemons admit they can hardly distinguish between the input from the Schlaich office and their own on many projects. Marg says: 'My relation to Jörg Schlaich is a dialogue between an architect who admires engineering and an engineer who admires

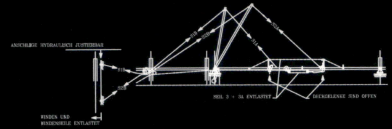

STAT. SYSTEM VERKEHRSLASTSTELLUNG

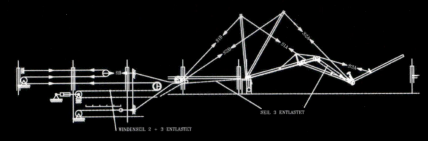

STAT. SYSTEM 0 BIS 15 GRAD

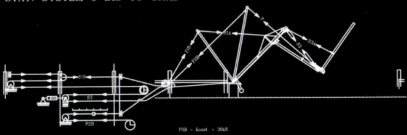

STAT. SYSTEM 15 BIS 90 GRAD

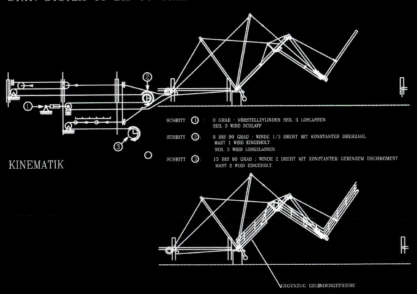

KINEMATIK

KINEMATIK GELÄNDER

sculptural kinetic art. The folding bridge is fairly common in maritime engineering in the form of the folding ramps of roll-on-roll-off cargo ships and the Kiel bridge has the traditional sea-bridge structure, resting on poles. Tests were carried out on a full-sized mock-up of the structure at Rostock Shipyard before the bridge was shipped to the site for erection. Constructed like an extending pontoon, the bridge represents the development of maritime port life at this crossing point.

Of his relationship with Jörg Schlaich, Marg writes:

> The synthesis is a kinetic sculpture, which gave both of us the joy of two boys playing just for fun. Our client did not have this feeling at all and watched our design work critically and with suspicion. We decided to carry out a forty-eight-hour test of the completed folding mechanism at the East German shipyard, where workers who would have otherwise had no job at the time made endless tests to demonstrate that even the rails would fold perfectly. We had to convince the client that even a combination of gale and thick ice would not affect the proper function. Now the public is happy and amused by this little kinetic masterpiece, but Jörg and I lost a lot of money as the fee was not sufficient. To put it bluntly: 'Innovation is an expensive experience.'[5]

12.5 above
Kiel Hörn Bridge, 1997: testing the structure at Rostock Shipyard

architecture. We find our solutions in a dialogue that is dominated by listening.'[4]

Also like Wilkinson Eyre (see Chapter 13), Marg has a keen interest in the integration of structure and services within architectural design. Nowhere is this more in evidence than at the Hanover Trade Fair, where a double-layered façade (not dissimilar to the double-layered timber hull of the *Activ*!) enables an environmentally sustainable and energy-saving solution. In order to locate services in the roof space, the scheme involved the use of glass ducts, which required close collaboration with environmental engineers.

No project more strikingly illustrates Marg's love for docks and shipping than the bridge at Kiel Hörn, which consists of an innovative three-part tension-folding bridge that enables ships to pass through as it folds back like a crane. The idea behind the bridge was to combine architecture, engineering and

12.6 left
Sketch drawings of the bridge's movement

12.4 right
The model simulates every stage of the bridge's folding movement

12.7
**Kiel Hörn Bridge, 1997:
the bridge folding**

Notes

1   A. Brookes and C. Grech (1992) *Connections: studies in building assemby*, London: Butterworth-Heinemann.

2   C. Slessor (2000) 'Pavilion of Christian Religions', *Architectural Review*, vol. 208, no. 1243, September, pp.78–9.

3   J. Zukowsky (1997) *The Architecture of Von Gerkan, Marg & Partners*, Munich, New York: Prestel Verlag.

4   V. Marg, letter to the authors, 2002.

5   V. Marg, letter to the authors, 2002.

Chapter 13

The incredible lightness of being

Chris Wilkinson, Wilkinson Eyre Architects

13.1
Dyson Headquarters, Malmesbury, 1999: entry to the building is via a glass bridge over a purple pool that reflects light onto a fabric canopy overhead (architect: Wilkinson Eyre Architects)

13.2
Explore at Bristol, 1999: the 15-metre-diameter stainless-steel sphere sits half in the water (architect: Wilkinson Eyre Architects)

Lightness is not a technical term and cannot be measured in a finite way. It can be neither quantified nor specified but is a qualitative ingredient of modern architecture that is gaining momentum – and it is a quality I strive for.

The concept of 'lightness' concerns the physical weight and property of materials, but it relates as much to the visual appearance of structures, components and even spaces. It is a quality that comes from form, composition and economical use of materials. It also relates closely to light and the way light is treated. Light in itself is a fundamental aspect of architecture, which probably reflects our innate instinct for survival, since we cannot exist without it. It follows, therefore, that buildings and structures, which control light, are pleasing to us.

Poets muse on the way light plays on water and there is something romantic about the reflections and the dancing movements that come from ripples on the surface. Water can have a powerful impact on architecture by transmitting light and reflecting it onto adjacent surfaces. The magical experience of Venice with its beautiful palazzos reflected in the canals on a sunny day has inspired architects of past and current generations to incorporate water into their designs. Reflecting pools can add lightness and interest.

This led us to design the purple pool in front of the entrance to the Dyson Headquarters at Malmesbury and the long rectangular pool at Explore at Bristol, which reflects the arcade and the planetarium. Both succeed in enhancing the architecture with ever-changing light reflections.

Similar qualities come from the play of light on the surfaces of different materials and form is enhanced by the contrasting of light and shade. Curved surfaces deal with light in an appealing way and a curved form will generally appear lighter than a corresponding square or rectangular form of the same volume. Projections and articulations pick up shadows and it is for this reason that traditional mouldings and decorative cornice details serve to enhance the appearance of heavy masonry buildings of the past.

Transparent and translucent materials also play with light in an interesting way. Glass is an abundant material in our lives but it still holds almost magical qualities for us. Its crystalline nature catches the light and sparkles like jewels. Glass buildings, however, can appear either light and transparent or solid and monumental depending on the lighting conditions at the time of day. Transparency, by definition, allows

space and light through, and seems to offer the kind of freedom that people want. We like to be able to experience the comforts of the inside whilst still enjoying the delights of the outside. We need light from the sun and we like to see it moving round throughout the day, for it helps us to orientate ourselves and to define time. So it follows that buildings which offer this 'light freedom' can be described as possessing lightness. Equally, materials, structures and building forms that deal with light in a pleasing way can be said to have 'lightness'.

For the principal façade of our Stratford Station in London, we chose to design a tension-structure-supported glazed wall with lightness in mind. The main structure, which is inclined at an angle of 11 degrees to the vertical, consists of an 8-metre-deep steel truss spanning three bays of 30 metres. It is constructed of CHS steel, shaped verticals at the top and bottom with purpose-designed ovoid tubes at 6-

13.3
Stratford Station, London, May 1999: the interior lighting reflects off the curved ceiling behind (architect: Wilkinson Eyre Architects)

13.4
The tension-structure-supported glazing has a delicate lightness

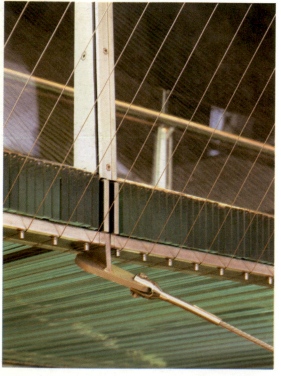

metre centres braced by steel rods. A secondary structure of stainless-steel rods and bracketry supports the glazing with proprietary bolted connections. The resultant appearance is one of filigree lightness, which contrasts with the clean, smooth curvature of the concourse soffit, and at night this 90-metre-long façade acts like a lightbox with reflected light from inside.

Tension structures invariably look lighter than compression structures and the elements of a structure that take tension forces are usually slimmer and lighter in weight. It is for this reason that they intrigue me and I would like to explain two examples in which we have explored the concept of lightness through the use of tension structures.

In the first example the brief to design a bridge across the atrium of the Science Museum in London as part of the 'Challenge of Materials Gallery' provided an ideal project to work through some ideas on tensegrity and responsive structures. Working with the engineer Bryn Bird, we set about designing a bridge spanning 16 metres to be constructed with the minimum amount of structural material.

In our first design session I brought an image of a spider's web and a postcard of a sculpture by the Australian artist Ken Unsworth called *Stone Circles II*, and Bryn brought a slide of the Gossamer Albatross – the first man-powered flight machine – and a glass sculpture by Danny Lane. He also referred to a structure he had designed for London Zoo in which multiple strands of very fine high-tensile cable were used. With this meeting of minds, the dialogue moved swiftly into a design in which a deck of laminated glass plates standing on edge was supported by an array of high-tensile steel cables, so fine as to be almost invisible – like a spider's web.

The weight of the deck helps to stabilize the structure but it was important that the loads were evenly distributed amongst the cables. Each cable was only 1.5 millimetres in diameter and was roughly capable of taking the load of one person. Much

13.5
The Challenge of Materials Bridge at the Science Museum, London, 1997: a glass deck suspended from an array of fine, high-tensile steel cables (architect: Wilkinson Eyre Architects)

13.6
Base detail showing laminated glass deck supported by cables fixed to a small stainless-steel channel

13.7
Head detail showing the 1.5-millimetre cables with piano key fixings for ease of tensioning

discussion took place on how to tension up the structure, which always led to comparisons with musical instruments, so it was perhaps not surprising that we ended up with a 'piano key' device to fine-tune the tension load on each cable. However, Bryn's suggestion that the bridge should be tuned with a guitar was rejected by the contractor in favour of a tension meter.

There were still problems with the construction process and I was alarmed about the 'jelly-like' feel of the bridge until the glass balustrade was fixed, which finally stiffened up the whole structure. This made me appreciate the beauty of a true tensegrity structure, which relies on each component doing its job to the full. This project was not without its risks but all those involved felt that the solution justified the tremendous effort that went into it.

In a similar way the Air Pavilion at our Magna

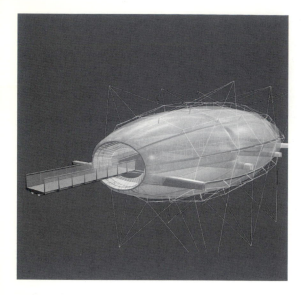

13.8
Magna Air Pavilion, Templeborough, 2001: computer image of translucent ETFE pillow fabric supported by tension cables (architect: Wilkinson Eyre Architects)

13.9
The translucent fabric enclosure glows with light in contrast to the surrounding dark space

project pushes the boundaries with a tension-supported, pillow fabric enclosure. Here our concept was for an airship-type structure hanging in the roof space of the gigantic, redundant Templeborough Steel Reprocessing Plant as part of a Millennium-funded, themed visitor attraction. The pavilion consists of a steel deck supported from the main building structure, connected by a bridge walkway to a vertical circulation core and enclosed with a lightweight, double-curvature skin of translucent ETFE (ethyltetrafluoroethylene) fabric that is inflated like pillows. The design was carried out with Atelier 10 and Ben Morris of Vector, who was also responsible for the fabrication and erection. The pillows, which stretch horizontally from one end to the other, are secured by aluminium extrusions and the overall shape is held in place by external tension cables fixed back to the main structure. This cable solution was chosen in preference to a compression-ring structure for reasons of economy but the resultant design also possesses the quality of lightness we wanted in contrast to the dark, heavy interior space of the steelworks building.

The lightness of tension structures is also noticeable in bridges, where long spans are required,

and in particular suspension bridges, where the slenderness of the deck and the apparent thinness of the supporting cables are accentuated by the scale of their horizontal spans. For us, this point was emphasized in our competition design for a footbridge across the Seine at the Parc de Bercy in Paris. Working with the engineer Chris Wise, we were able to achieve a span of 200 metres with cables of only 180 millimetres diameter, onto which the deck was seated. This minimal structure relied on a cable sag of 6 metres between supports and huge anchor bearings at each end, taking loads of 9,000 tonnes from the cables. The incredible visual lightness of the structure is compensated for only by the considerable unseen foundations, which are possible in Paris because of the rock substructure.

However it is not only suspension bridges that possess the attributes of visual lightness. We have learned ways of making our structures look as light as possible through design. For example, our Gateshead Millennium Bridge, which spans over 100 metres and weighs 1,000 tons, still looks quite delicate. This has been achieved by carefully shaping the steel arch structure to catch the light in such a way as to reduce its visual bulk. The section, which

13.10
Bercy Bridge, Paris, 1999: competition entry for a 200-metre-span footbridge over the Seine with 180-millimetre cables

13.11
Gateshead Millennium Bridge, 2001: section of the arch structure in the fabrication works
Guy Hearn, photo used with kind permission from Gateshead Council

13.12 left
Gateshead Millennium Bridge, 2001: the constantly changing section of the arch has been designed to catch the light and reduce the structure's visual bulk

13.14 above
The translucent composite cladding on the south elevation of Stratford Market depot provides a glowing light like the Japanese *shogi*

13.13 right
Stratford Market Depot, London, 1999: the articulation of the structure and materials combined with its acute angle creates lightness

changes along its length, is shaped to deal with the forces applied to it and is tapered to a sharp edge on one side. This carefully worked-out profile reduces in depth towards the top of the arch where it looks much slimmer. It is a trick that we learned on our Hulme Arch Bridge in Manchester, which also consisted of a parabolic arch with a constantly changing tapered steel section. Both bridges benefit from the play of light and shade upon the structure, and the cost of fabrication was not exorbitant because of the computerized cutting techniques employed by the manufacturers from Watson Steel.

In an entirely different way our Stratford Market Depot for the Jubilee Line Extension achieves lightness through design, even though it requires a substantial structure to enclose the huge space, which measures 100 x 190 metres. Here the steelwork is fabricated out of circular sections with tapered ends and is clearly articulated from the building skin. The glazed end wall, which turns past the corner to give transparency, and the cantilevered floor structure, both contribute to the feeling of lightness.

The detailing of the supporting windframe structure, together with the choice of materials for the south elevation, goes some way to achieving a similar delicacy and lightness to a Naum Gabo sculpture. Here the proprietary translucent fibreglass composite cladding, known as 'Kallwall', was used to provide daylight without solar gain and the effect of the 100-metre-long uninterrupted wall is rather like the traditional Japanese *shogi*. The supporting structure is composed of cell-form beams, braced with yacht-rigging cables, which provide the visual lightness we required.

Many of these images serve to explain another aspect of our design vocabulary, which is the clear expression of structure and function. For us it isn't enough for the structure to work, it also has to look as though it works properly. We always try to separate the major elements, allowing them full expression, and we pay careful attention to the way they are joined together.

Lightness also plays a part in the design of our Dyson Headquarters Building. Here two vast industrial sheds housing the design, administration, production and storage facilities are separated by a small glazed pavilion, which forms the entrance to both buildings. The lightweight structure and crystalline transparency of its enclosure give it a lightness that contrasts with the mass of the adjoining buildings.

This is further emphasized by a fabric canopy in front that floats above the reflecting pool, which contains a light sculpture by the artist Diana Edmunds. This sculpture, based on the concept of long willowy reeds swaying in the breeze, conveys the very essence of lightness since it is composed of acrylic rods that have been abraded to refract the daylight and glow at night when lit with fibre optics from below.

In their recently published book, *Lightness*, Adriaan Beukers and Ed van Hinte, from the Faculty of Aerospace Engineering at Delft University of Technology, refer to 'the inevitable renaissance of minimum-energy structures'. For them lightness is concerned not just with buildings or aeroplanes, but with 'the structure of all things made and grown'. Their main message is 'the lighter the better', which follows on from Buckminster Fuller's dictum of 'more with less'. But in architecture lightness is not only about weight but also about appearance. Perhaps a better description is supplied by Professor Alan Brookes, who referred to Milan Kundera's book *The Unbearable Lightness of Being*.

13.15
Dyson Headquarters, 'Lightreeds' by Diana Edmunds in the reflecting pool convey the very essence of lightness

13.16
Dyson Headquarters, Malmesbury, 1999: the entrance building – a glazed pavilion that contrasts with the bulk of the adjacent production sheds

Index

Index

Index